warning.

What is Mark Stevens talking about? My company sucks? Maybe *his* does. But who the hell is he to mouth off like that?

Good questions. They're the same ones I (Mark Stevens) would ask. So I guess, given that I started this, I have to answer them, and I will. I've always been advised not to start what I couldn't finish.

But allow me to issue this warning first: the truth in these pages is going to come at you like a blast from a double-barrel shotgun—so brace yourself. I am writing this book because, in the past, my company has sucked. And it will suck again if I don't make damn certain that there is a near-religious zeal in our company culture to achieve excellence—to provide a thrilling experience for the customer—so much so that I am utterly dissatisfied if I fail to hit the standard I'm on a mission to achieve. I, like you, must be forever restless, relentless, and driven. I have seen my company go from sucking to soaring, and I want to help you get there, too.

As the CEO of a marketing and management consulting firm, my job is to speed the upward trajectory and reverse the down cycles of my company's clients' businesses. We work with companies of all sizes, in all stages of the business cycle:

- Startup
- Runaway growth

- Dead end
- Roadblock
- Slow decline
- Free fall

In the process, I see strong, smart, talented, gutsy, and creative men and women at the helm of their companies—each with their money and egos hanging in the balance—struggling at times to eliminate the flaws that threaten the enterprises they have built. Some are tottering on the brink of failure or heading into a downward spiral.

Interestingly, nearly all business managers I talk to believe the challenges and obstacles they face are unique. It's as if they are having an out-of-body experience that no one else has ever experienced in the history of commerce and capitalism. But they are *not* unique at all. Although it appears from a distance that there are a thousand reasons for a company's failings and shortcomings—all unique to the individual enterprises—the reasons, as different as they may appear to be on the surface, fall into four major categories:

1. Rudderless Leadership
2. The Lust-to-Lax Syndrome
3. Incompetence
4. Conventional Thinking

These four unhealthy traits manifest themselves in many forms and develop into a pattern that either never goes away or returns over and over again like an unrelenting plague. Let me expound a little on what each entails:

1. **Rudderless Leadership:** Management has lost command and control of the business. Employees act on the basis of their own agendas, are accountable to no one, engage in a set of actions that are random, disconnected, and devoid of a cohesive strategy. What looks like a company no longer qualifies for that distinction. It is better viewed as the reality of what it has become: a group of people working under the same roof but rarely, if ever, moving in the same direction.

2. **The Lust-to-Lax Syndrome:** Existing customers are taken for granted by a management team hyperfocused on attracting new business into its camp at the expense of those patrons who are the most loyal to it. In time, the former loyalists leave, frustrated by their stepchild status and the service that goes with it. That makes the business a leaky boat, with everyone bailing frantically to stay above water. New business is vital, but a company's most important and valuable asset is its customer base. Treat them with indifference and your company truly sucks.

3. **Incompetence.** They do not know how to generate return on investment (ROI) on their marketing initiatives. They spend on programs that fail to grow the business or (having reached the breaking point with marketing that barely moves the needle) they do nothing to grow the business at all. This preventive move *never* produces results. You don't make money by saving money; you make money by investing money wisely. Those who have stopped trying to make money through investing always have companies that are stuck in neutral.

4. **Conventional Thinking.** An aggressive competitor moves into the market and immediately seizes market share. The manager of the resident business complains about the "carpetbagger" but does little to defend the company's position. Anger and frustration lead not to a determination to succeed against any and all odds but to a devastating paralysis. The hard fact is that the free market is not *fair*—it is a competitive war zone where those who can face adversity, revise their strategy, and move forward always prevail over time. Move forward by thinking and acting in an innovative, even iconoclastic fashion. Don't be trapped by conventional thinking.

Fighting those patterns and understanding how to move beyond satisfying your customers to *thrilling* is what this book is all about. These pages will instruct you on:

- How to identify your company's negative qualities—you may have only one or you may have all four;
- When to stop blaming everyone and everything but yourself;
- What works to engineer U-turns in company performance and what fails because it is simply putting lipstick on a pig;
- How to know when you're in denial; and, most important,
- How to challenge convention and take the often drastic steps that need to become standard operating procedures at your company.

The goal, my fellow entrepreneurs and capitalists, is to put our companies into orbit for a lifetime of scalable and sustainable growth—to go from sucking to soaring. It's time to declare war against ourselves, to go on the offense to attack those areas that bring us down, and then launch our businesses skyward by captivating our customers—to thrill them so much they wouldn't dream of going anywhere else. Everything else is a treadmill to nowhere.

Your Company Sucks.

Praise for
Your Company Sucks

"*Your Company Sucks* is immediately useful and wildly inspirational (no matter what size business you run). Filled with practical ideas and entertaining stories, Mark Stevens helps you identify how your company sucks and gives you an action plan for doing a U-turn."

—REGIS HADIARIS, Creator of the Dot Connector Blog

"Mark Stevens offers a vitamin boost into the blood stream of business; an elixir for newbie entrepreneurs and war-weary tycoons alike."

—BEN KOETHER, Chairman and Founder of
Kitchen Brains

"I absolutely love this brutally honest and practical approach to business—and life. *Your Company Sucks* motivates me to sleep less because I am so excited about working on the many things in the book that ring true to me and need attention in my business. Bravo, Mark Stevens, on your courageous approach to being aware of the obvious and actually coming directly to the point about how to change for the better."

—JOSEPH ESSA, President of
Wolfgang Puck Worldwide, Inc.

"This is a book that every business owner needs to read. The challenges we face today in the world of commerce are clearly identified with brilliant clarity by Mark Stevens. Reading this is like having Mark personally guide you and your team through the process of identifying exactly where you are in the life of your company, and more importantly, what to do about it."

—DENNIS CURTIN, Regional Owner of
RE/MAX Mid-states & Dixie Region

Your Company Sucks makes every CEO who reads it take the time to stop, to think, and to act!"

—RICH PARLONTIERI, CEO and President of
Speedemissions, Inc.

Your Company Sucks.

It's Time to Declare War on Yourself

MARK STEVENS
CEO of MSCO Inc.
Author of *Your Marketing Sucks*

BenBella Books
Dallas, Texas

BenBella

BenBella Books, Inc.
10300 N. Central Expressway, Suite 400
Dallas, TX 75231
benbellabooks.com
Send feedback to feedback@benbellabooks.com

Printed in the United States of America
10 9 8 7 6 5 4 3 2 1

Library of Congress Cataloging-in-Publication Data is available for this title.
978-1935618546

Editing by Debbie Harmsen
Copyediting by Deb Kirkby
Proofreading by Michael Fedison
Cover design by Melody Cadungog
Text design and composition by Silver Feather Design
Printed by Berryville Graphics

Distributed by Perseus Distribution
(perseusdistribution.com)

Significant discounts for bulk sales are available. Please contact
Glenn Yeffeth at glenn@benbellabooks.com or (214) 750-3628.

Contents.

1.

Your Business Woes Are Keeping You Up at Night

You can't sleep at night. You're distracted when your spouse is talking to you. You're constantly looking over your shoulder as if someone is going to discover the dirty little secret you won't even say out loud to yourself—your company sucks. Shh! Someone might hear.

This stressful situation makes you miserable, frustrated, frightened, confused, and sometimes even ashamed and depressed. Not only are there sleepless nights, but there are anxious days, too—and all manner of second-guessing.

You are not sure how, why, or when it happened, but you know that somewhere along the way, something went terribly wrong with your business. The business you created to provide you with affluence and independence is now draining you emotionally and/or financially. Your livelihood, your investment, your pride, your baby is on the way to tanking (or consistently disappointing you) and you don't know how to stop it. And worse yet, instead of the freedom you believed a company of your own would provide, it enslaves you. You don't have a business—the business has you!

You know what I'm talking about. You are no longer the owner or manager of the business per se; you are its captive. You work long, hard hours, you try everything you can think of to improve the situation, but you know instinctively (and from those damn bank statements and the sullen look on your customers' faces) that you are sliding backwards. Your business is in jeopardy. Sometimes you want to deny it, as if ignoring it will make it go away. But you know better. It's time to pull the blinders off and face the truth.

Your business used to be more of a joy, not a burden, and was once a cash machine, not a financial drain. So the huge, hurtling meteor of a question you must ask yourself is, "What went wrong?"

First, remember the good old days—not to run from the pain but to look at how things used to be. Your business was not always the way it is now, not by a long shot. Your business used to be more of a joy, not a burden, and was once a cash machine, not a financial drain. So the huge, hurtling meteor of a question you must ask yourself is, "What went wrong?"

The answer, in the vast majority of cases, is actually quite simple (but nonetheless challenging): *your business adds up to less than the sum of its parts.* It does not fuse its people, products, services, and concepts into a unique entity with an exponent over its name. You may try hard. You may have good intentions. You may have all the elements the textbooks call for. But still your company suffers from an insidious form of slow death: it fails to *thrill.*

Deer in the Headlights

I know dead-on when a business owner is gripped by the knowledge that his company has slid off the rails. Though he tries to disguise it, and maybe succeeds in the face of his employees, I can read *the look* from a mile away. Think of it as a tired, confused, even panic-stricken gaze signaling that he is struggling with an issue. He has a secret of sorts. I say *of sorts* because the prospects who failed to transition into customers and those who bought in the past but have disappeared into the arms of competitors—they all know, at least intuitively, the dynamic at work at this fellow's company. They cannot be fooled. They see and sense the owner's desperation, his lack of confidence, his fear. That skittish behavior and deer-in-the-headlights look are terribly costly because of a powerful and generally unwritten rule of commerce—customers and clients are driven to do business with those who appear strong and robust

> *Customers and clients are driven to do business with those who appear strong and robust and conversely are repelled by those who appear shaky and weak.*

and conversely are repelled by those who appear shaky and weak.

Success breeds success and failure leads to disaster. Think of the crowded restaurant that everyone flocks to dine in. Complain and gripe as you may about the long waits, you'll be back over and over again because the food is so delicious and the atmosphere draws you in. And if everyone is coming here, it must be a great place. It is strong and robust.

Play this scenario against the quiet restaurant, nearly empty, a patron or two seated at its fifty tables. The host, though pleasant enough, takes a while to seat you, and the server forgets your extra lemon. Or maybe he seats you right away, but it's like he's trying too hard. His eyes are almost pleading, "Like me, like me!" Something in your gut says, "This place sucks. It's a loser. How can I get out of here without insulting the guy?"

Like every person at the helm of a company on the skids, the lonely and desperate restaurateur knows something is terribly wrong. He just doesn't want to say it out loud, to admit it to himself in the bright glare of daylight. It's as if keeping silent will somehow limit the damage.

The poorly kept secret is that his company is exhibiting one or more of the four characteristics that lead to failure that I mentioned in the warning at the beginning of this book, and his business is suffering as a result:

- It fails to truly excite people about its products or services and to keep them intoxicated—it has the Lust-to-Lax Syndrome.

- It is rife with internal conflict, driven by cabals among employees who have developed their own agendas and who fail to follow the leader's strategy (if there is a leader or a strategy at all—this falls under the Rudderless Leadership category).

- It's a ship adrift, going through the motions, filling orders but doing so in a haphazard way. It lacks direction and the internal combustion to drive it to the winner's circle—again, failed leadership is at work here along with incompetence and conventional thinking.

- Worst of all—and this is the hardest part of the secret for the owner or manager to admit—the company is actually on a trajectory that will lead to its demise or endless pursuit of success that proves to be elusive. Most likely, the business is stuck in neutral or locked in reverse, with revenues failing to grow or diminishing month by month, year by year. If a dramatic change is not made, the enterprise will go out of business, producing zero equity or income for the person who built it. This painful fact of life is often camouflaged until the defects that threaten the business are so egregious and inflamed that the end is near and the options for reversing the decline are few, challenging, and costly.

A Bedtime Story

Let's examine the case of a highly recognized company that once had the status and stature of a market leader, a finely managed and operated business, that allowed itself to deteriorate, fall on its face, and lose its way. Consider it a perfect example of a company that sucked. Although your company may not be the size of this major corporation, the lessons from its example are valuable for small businesses, too. The sins it committed are replicated every day by other companies—yours doesn't have to be one of them.

The business in question is Holiday Inn. Founded in 1952 by Kemmons Wilson, the hotel chain proved to be an instant American success story. It was on a trip away from home that Wilson had an epiphany: travelers did not have a place to stay the night—a hotel or motel brand—that offered a reliable level of quality. Drive up to a lodgings establishment and it could turn out to be anything from a clean and homey inn presided over by a doting retired couple to a nightmarish one resembling the Bates Motel.

Wilson was determined to change that by opening hotels that would be clean, value-priced, family-friendly, and accessible from major roadways. And he wanted to do this for every Holiday Inn location, making each establishment virtually identical and thus reliably similar. This visionary entrepreneur from Memphis launched the first four Holiday Inns in or on the outskirts of Elvis's hometown in 1953. His concept struck a chord with the American psyche and proved to be an instant success. Fifteen years after the Memphis debut, there were a thousand Holiday Inns dotting the U.S. landscape, and when the company made the cover of *Time* in 1972, the chain had mushroomed to 1,400 inns.

I grew up with Holiday Inns; you might have as well. As an adolescent, I would stay at the inns with my family on our road trips in and around the Eastern Seaboard. And as a college kid, I would pick the familiar and affordable option when I wanted to get away with a girlfriend.

I was a middle-class kid, so money was always a factor, but none of us (my parents, girlfriends, or I) wanted to sleep in a dump. We knew we weren't in the lap of luxury (to be honest, we really didn't know what luxe was), but we (and millions like us) flocked to Holiday Inns because the chain consistently gave us what we wanted at a price we could afford.

And then the founding family sold the business (first Holiday Inn International in 1988 and then North American Holiday Inn in 1990) to UK-based Bass LLC, the beer-makers and parent company of InterContinental Hotels Group PLC. Under this new leadership, everything Holiday Inn was when it took America by storm evaporated under a management team that appeared to have little or no respect for, or understanding of, what the company represented.

Under the new management's neglectful stewardship, the Holiday Inn experience became sloppy, unpredictable, worn, and tired, both in look and in welcome (or lack of one).

The company declined from a great value to a cheap stay. Furnishings were dated, paint jobs were delayed, signage was often broken or poorly lit, and training (what was left of it) did more to keep patrons away than to provide the family feeling that lends a lodging facility a sense of being a home away from home. This was a sea change and a highly unattractive one at that—so much so that on a business trip during the early stages of my career, I decided to sleep in my car rather than accept the fleabag room a Holiday Inn night manager showed me.

Without Wilson's vision and with high standards out of the picture—replaced by operations geeks and financial engineers—Holiday Inn became a company that sucked virtually across the board. Revenues, profit, and customer satisfaction all took it on the chin. A once-great American enterprise was a shadow of its old self.

This happens when inept management in any field or industry and in any size of company forgets:

- That it's essential to live by the brand's promise;
- That the customer's loyalty has to be fought for—if it's not, the customer can easily be drawn away by other choices;
- That as important as it is to be fiscally prudent, you cannot put your brand in danger by allowing your product or service to deteriorate. Saving money may generate a short-term boost in profitability, but it's often at the expense of the company's viability.

The extent of the malaise at Holiday Inn in its dark days comes into sharper focus when you consider the scope of the turnaround initiated in 2007:

- Total cost: $1 billion plus;
- 3,400 hotels and 430,000 rooms renovated;
- Completely revamped guest welcome experience;
- Redesigned brand image and signage;
- Upgraded bedding, pillows, and linens to provide an all-important residential look and feel; and the
- Implementation of a "Stay Real" training program to assure guest expectations are exceeded once again.

In summary, in 2007, Holiday Inn declared war on itself and it proved to be a win-win for guests and stakeholders as satisfaction and financial performance levels rose substantially.

My Own Pounding Headache: The Migraine Born from Mediocrity

It feels awful to run a company that sucks—to wake up at night and stare at the ceiling, knowing something is terribly wrong. I think of it as *Migraine Misérable*.

I know the pain and anguish of this from firsthand experience. I brought it on myself and had no one to blame but Mark Stevens. That was the bad news. The good news is that I learned from it.

None of my observations on the state of a troubled business (or one that will soon be categorized as such) are academic. The primary driver and source of my insights and guidance are based on personal experiences. Think of it as a veritable punch in the solar plexus, stemming from the painful truth that I founded and managed a business that once failed to measure up. I had to look in the unforgiving mirror and admit I had somehow taken a wrong turn and ended up in Sucksville.

When I started my marketing firm in 1995, I had no idea how to run a business based on my hybrid vision of marketing and management consulting. I was inventing on the run, in real time, and driving over speed bumps en route to the success I was determined to achieve.

At first, I thought I had it all packaged up for guaranteed success. I created a powerful methodology for growing companies based on the belief that there is a universal equation that will drive revenues and profitability. I framed it as C+A+M=PG (Capture Customers + Augment Your Relationship with Them + Maintain Them for Life = Perpetual Growth).

I was a student of physics, loving the way giants of science such as Newton boiled complex dynamics into simple rules and principles (e.g., "a body in motion tends to stay in motion") and believed I could do the same for business. That is, create a grand unified theory for growing companies so management can focus on only a few key leverage points as opposed to hundreds of moving parts. Thus, C + A + M = PG was born.

So I had a road map, and I was assembling a strong team, but there were some glaring weaknesses that I did not address—I didn't realize at first how big these shortcomings were. I believed at the time that they were insignificant against the background of my strategic achievements, but I was dreadfully wrong. My company sucked. At least once a week, a client would tell me so. "Mark, you're a smart guy and we like working with you, but, Mark, nothing is ever delivered the day you say it will be. Deadlines are missed. Schedules are blown. Your team makes promises and then breaks them."

That cut me to the quick—doubly so because I knew that it was true. No one at MSCO was a bad person or intentionally failed to deliver on time and in full, but we were performing like losers, and that's all that mattered to clients.

Here, precisely, is what I saw in the mirror: a reflection of what a company looks like when it sucks. I winced every time a client called to complain, but I didn't act—not quickly enough. I gave employees second, third, and even fourth chances. I wanted to save them. I wanted everything to work out. This was based not on a belief that business can ever be a democracy (I never fell victim to that) but instead on a more damaging (and widely held) faith I think of as "Hope Springs Eternal." This fantasy leads to the false conclusion, the Hollywood ending, that everything will just magically work out. It rarely does, but I was lost in the fantasy and in a misguided belief that my employees were at the root of the problem, and that they would somehow see the light, correcting all the issues.

*Problems and
defects don't cure
themselves. They
fester and compound,
marching the business
inexorably toward
deterioration and
destruction. It's up to
you as the leader to
take charge.*

But when you face the facts, if you are going to engineer a turnaround you must admit that when you're in Sucksville, it isn't anyone's fault but your own. Problems and defects don't cure themselves. They fester and compound, marching the business inexorably toward deterioration and destruction. It's up to you as the leader to take charge. You must declare war on yourself.

REALITY CHECK: DOES YOUR COMPANY SUCK?

At this point, you may be wondering if your company really does suck. You suspect so, but how do you know if it's truly dysfunctional or performing below its potential? It's not that surprising, to me at least, that you lack a reliable answer. You could be in denial or maybe you just aren't sure how your company ranks on the performance meter—and in fact, you may have never even thought of rating the business this way before.

If you experience any of the following telltale signs, the time has come to recognize that your business is failing to measure up and is in need of immediate—perhaps drastic—action:

- You don't sleep well at night due to business issues you may not be able to put your finger on. The questions are many, but the answers aren't clear. You know something is wrong, but the source of the problem is evading you, gnawing at you.

- Employees don't seem to respect you or the company. They do their own thing, having little joy in their jobs.

- Your sales manager keeps beating a dead horse. The sales team isn't meeting quotas, and so when the manager takes them out to the woodshed, he puts the fear of God in them one day and then gives Knute Rockne pep talks the next. But in the end, sales are flat and the sales team is confused, upset, and disillusioned.

- Everybody thinks they are underpaid.

- Your products and services are so commoditized that customers and prospects are totally focused on cutting prices. For some reason, you stopped innovating or acquiring exciting, innovative products and your company is suffering because of it.

- You are blindly following conventional wisdom even though it is leading you down a slippery slope (see my blog, "Unconventional Thinking" at www.msco.com).

Clearly, the time has come to act.

2.

Effective Leaders Create Good Company Cultures

At the beginning of this book, in the Warning section, I recounted four reasons why businesses fail:

1. Rudderless Leadership
2. The Lust-to-Lax Syndrome
3. Incompetence
4. Conventional Thinking

This chapter looks at the first—rudderless leadership—in more detail to help you pinpoint why and where your company is weak. We start with leadership because it drives everything else.

Follow the Leader

Skilled managers recognize that the company's ability to outperform all expectations, virtually all of the time, sits squarely in their wheelhouse. As such, they never rely on a single rule or policy to ensure that products are manufactured or that services are delivered according to plan, to the highest standards, and on budget. Instead, they set up a system of redundancy that sets off fail-safe checks and balances when one or more of the quality steps is missed or ignored.

It's like a parachute. It has a backup built in that you can open if the primary ripcord fails. This precaution is based on a healthy sense of skepticism that even the best-laid plans will actually come to pass as intended.

In a typical case of blind faith driving a company down the tubes, a prominent restaurant company asked my firm to add firepower to its marketing, shaken as it was by the failure of its new barbeque chain to catch on in the marketplace.

Before we would engage in any form of marketing, we insisted on testing the product, visiting the restaurants unaccompanied by management in order to make sure the food and service were not being upgraded due to the presence of VIPs on the scene. Even though we visited with an open mind (meaning we didn't let the chef's world-class reputation color our assessment of the experience), what we found surprised us: the food at the barbecue restaurants was third-rate at best.

This took management by surprise because they:

1. Believed their quality control manager (who was tasked with making certain that the food met the highest standards), who constantly asserted, as revealed in detailed reports, that everything was up to snuff. A respected manager provided comforting reports on the state of the business, only for management to discover that the reports weren't worth the paper they were printed on. How could this happen? Because no system of redundant quality control was put in place to make sure the reports had validity. Without a redundant system in place, the quality guy could spend his days playing video games, issuing reassuring reports, and no one would know the difference. The fact is, management must insist on a way to check on the person providing the input on the level of quality/standard of performance. Without this, it is like asking your controller how much money is in the corporate account without ever seeing the bank reports.

> *Management must insist on a way to check on the person providing the input on the level of quality/standard of performance. Without this, it is like asking your controller how much money is in the corporate account without ever seeing the bank reports.*

If you want proof of how risky that can be, ask Bernie Madoff's victims.

2. Never ate the food themselves. The first rule of management is constantly to take the role of a) the lowest ranking employee in your business and b) your customers. Forget the focus groups, management re-treats, status reports, and blah, blah, blah. Rolling up your sleeves and getting into the soup now and then is the only way to know if the business sings or if it sucks.

WHY ASK WHY?

Do you fail to ask yourself *Why? Why* is the most im-portant word in business. I don't mean the everyday *why* bandied about in dozens of conversations about insignificant issues. I mean grand, sweeping *whys* that, when explored, investigated, and answered honestly (and held accountable by redundant checks and balanc-es), can reveal deep and critical flaws in the business:

•   Why do we keep making or stocking slow-moving products? Are we doing a poor job of marketing/selling them or are they no longer in demand? Do we need to make a wholesale change in our product lines?

- Why do we think it is so important to be specialists? Generalists? Would we be better off reversing our current focus?

- Why is our pricing structured as it is? Can we afford to raise our prices and thus generate higher margins? Or are we stuck in a legacy pricing model that predates the Internet and is too high?

- Why do we make it hard for customers to do business with us? Do we even know if it is hard or a total pleasure?

How should you deal with the *whys*? How should you address them in the course of your busy day? I suggest that you (as I do) set aside a quiet period for this critical reflection.

The most important time of the day for a business owner/manager is the few minutes before she falls asleep. As she rewinds the day, she is disturbed/concerned or exhilarated by any number of issues. In the process, the *whys* creep into her thinking. Although we are all tempted to glide off to sleep and put these uncertainties on hold, this is precisely the time (difficult as it may be) to issue a promissory note to yourself that you will act on the *whys* in the morning. Write it on a Post-it note or an iPad tablet computer that you keep by your bed and be prepared to get answers to the *whys* in the coming days. If I am too beat to focus on it when an important *why* slips into my brain, I like to set the alarm for an hour earlier and get right to it when my thinking is fresh and there is an urgency to it.

WHAT TO LOOK FOR

Do any of your employees:

- Have agendas of their own and believe they are free to pursue them, even if the actions they take run counter to the strategy you have established? (I am taking a leap of faith that you have established a clear and concise strategy and that you have informed your team of it.)

- Have an entitlement sensibility that tells them that they should be handsomely rewarded in salary and benefits, regardless of their level of performance?

- Exhibit a form of corporate cancer, turning their co-workers against the company? (These losers create stealth unions or cabals that must be crushed.) Every time you look in the mirror, admit there's a cancer in the ranks, and surgically remove it, you liberate yourself and your team—and you find within days that you have a better company in far better position to respond to your goals and to thrill your customers.

As leaders, the question we must come to grips with is why we allow these blind spots to cloud and distort our field of vision, marring our companies' performance or, at the very least, leaving us myopic about their shortcomings.

Perhaps we'd do best to look to a man who was a small business owner in Kansas City before he was elevated to the presidency of the United States: Harry S. Truman.

When Truman famously said, "The buck stops here," he likely didn't realize that he was providing businesspeople with profound, albeit hard-to-swallow, advice. The failure to live up to *that* Truman doctrine by accepting personal responsibility for the performance and excellence of our companies is the primary reason businesses that perform poorly find themselves in that unenviable position. When the company becomes lax, dysfunctional, complacent, balkanized—when it fails to thrill and leaves its customers disappointed or heading for the hills—it is always because of the boss's failure to identify weaknesses and address them decisively.

"The Buck Stops Here" Test

How well do you follow the Truman perspective? Decide if you see yourself in the following profile: You always look for scapegoats to take the heat when things go wrong. A strategy falls apart at the seams, a major customer threatens to cancel her relationship with your firm due to a serious flaw in the services delivered, and your knee-jerk conclusion is that your employees are at fault. You say they dropped the ball, they failed to anticipate the risks, they allowed the customer service policy to unwind.

Ah, how convenient it is to shift blame, to free yourself of the burden of responsibility; however, in doing so, you are setting the wheels in motion for a repeat performance—and then another. You have failed the "The Buck Stops Here" test. You are refusing to admit that you failed to set the policies and procedures designed to prevent these mishaps. It's clearly time to declare war on yourself.

Incompetence in the Wings: A Leader's Exit Strategy that is a Trap Door in Disguise

The situation is all too familiar to me and my team. A businessperson strides into my office with a request to develop a marketing initiative *immediately* or to extinguish an organizational fire. Before we can act intelligently, we need to identify and understand these root causes ("Ready. Fire. Aim." never works). As we talk through the request and the reasons behind it, the discussion evolves into an archeological dig of a commercial enterprise buried under years of flawed practices, pretenses, and levels of bureaucracy no one knows who started and what value (if any) they add. Someplace beneath the surface lie the real roots of the issues at hand.

The truth is revealed in the following stages:

1. Let's assume the business owner wants to play a less active role in the company and plans to hand over the reins gradually to a highly competent employee, who will be mentored, positioned, and prepared to buy her out. The owner states that everything is moving along according to plan, but something (she can't put her finger on it) doesn't feel exactly right.

2. As we reverse engineer from the goal of a succession plan to the devil that is always in the details, it becomes abundantly clear that the would-be successor is hardly up to the task of running the business. In fact, as he has assumed ever-greater responsibility, the business has faltered, with revenues and profits declining. This is due in great measure to the fact that he has absolutely no feel for customers; instead of building relationships, his incompetence in this area has led to a significant (and clearly worrisome) exodus of once-loyal customers.

3. After some prodding, the company president admits that she knows of her lieutenant's weaknesses but is confident ("Well,"

she admits, "pretty confident") that he can close the knowledge and experience gaps with the proper training and incentives. And in one audacious and unwarranted leap of faith, she is certain that in short order she can enjoy the fruits of her exit strategy (when the successor buys her out).

4. In the midst of this fantasy (and it is amazing how much the perverse power of "hope springs eternal" damages businesses), the slide in the company's financial performance continues, customer relationships deteriorate further, and politically motivated cabals divide the company's personnel into warring camps, virtually all of whom feel that the business is rudderless. And, in a sense, it is: the owner is easing her way out (according to an exit plan based mostly on wishful thinking) at the same time that the successor is proving himself incapable of filling the gap. You spell that scenario B-l-a-c-k H-o-l-e.

There is a void in the business. Why? Because no one is truly in charge. Both the owner and the heir apparent are hoping for the impossible—that some divine force, perhaps a marketing blitz or just plain luck or momentum, will intercede and allow mediocrity to fill in where once there was an entrepreneurial force driving the business forward. The gap this creates leaves employees and customers to fend for themselves.

Every business in this state of affairs sucks. Why? Because leadership is never an option; it is a requirement for scalable and sustainable growth. And simply calling someone a leader, a president, or a managing director does not make her one. She must have the experience, the instincts, and the DNA for it, or the entire structure will fall on its face, taking the exit strategy or the goal of continuous growth along with it.

When that business owner visited me, her instincts were telling her what her brain did not want to process (another common reason companies lose their edge). As a result, she was under tremendous stress because she had one foot out the door of the enterprise she'd built and one foot in. She wanted to work less and play more, but as she did so, she saw the fault lines in sharp relief. The business was suffering, customers were complaining, employees were bickering, the value of the entity was slumping and later nose-diving. In this dangerous scenario, even if the designated successor could buy out the company, the valuation would be less than half (or much worse) of what it was worth when the exit plan was initially hatched.

No one is truly in charge. Both the owner and the heir apparent are hoping for the impossible—that some divine force, perhaps a marketing blitz or just plain luck or momentum, will intercede and allow mediocrity to fill in where once there was an entrepreneurial force driving the business forward.

Clearly, the fact that the exit strategy was a trap door in disguise was now obvious to the company's owner. Her preference to look the other way is not at all uncommon.

One of the primary—and in fact, most painful (because it is so easily remedied)—reasons companies wind up going south in terms of operating and financial performance is because management refuses to accept what is staring directly and ominously in its face. In this case, the president found it far more pleasant to dream about the multiple rewards of the buyout strategy than to come to grips with the fact that her company was deteriorating and that its mounting difficulties could be traced, in good measure, to the leadership gap she created.

The president found it far more pleasant to dream about the multiple rewards of the buyout strategy than to come to grips with the fact that her company was deteriorating.

It fell to me to rain on her parade, advising her in no uncertain terms that the only legitimate option at her disposal was to forget the exit for now, shut the trapdoor, re-enter the business, and reclaim control. Once the company was thrilling again, we could reconnect with an exit strategy—this time, with the goods to claim a high premium for her shares.

Culture Can Be Cancer

If your company is performing below its potential, chances are good that *culture* is one of the root causes of the malaise. Culture falls under leadership because as a leader you set the tone at your workplace.

Before we delve into this, allow me to put the subject in context. You're likely weary of the term *culture* and for good reason. There's a lot of talk about corporate culture, most of it hot air, pumped through the halls of business schools, where no one knows anything about the realities of actual business vs. make-believe textbook business. Harvard professors have written tomes on culture, but most of them have never run a business of any kind, so you can feel free to ignore their endless reams of gobbledygook.

That said, we shouldn't allow the academic boneheads to diminish the importance of culture in managing our companies.

I am concerned with culture because getting your company's culture right is among the most important things you can do, and talking about it won't do the trick. Often, it's just the opposite. I hear speeches, seminars, entire conventions focused on culture, matched in equal measure by a dearth of action. There is too much talk of culture without sufficient substance to support its actual role in your company's performance. Part of the problem is how culture is defined. So, what do I mean by *culture*?

There is too much talk of culture without sufficient substance to support its actual role in your company's performance. That said, we shouldn't allow the academic boneheads to diminish the importance of culture in managing our companies.

The best definition of culture is reflected in a deceptively simple axiom: "Culture is what the employees do when the boss *isn't* watching."

A great example came to me as I was writing this book. One day, I sat down for a very late lunch (4 p.m.) at a joint called The Route 22 Diner in Armonk, New York. It was a bitter January day, the tail end of the New Year's weekend. The sky was steel gray, the roads were patched with black ice, and most of the town residents were still away on vacation, skiing in Vail or sunning in Barbados.

I could tell when I entered the informal, cozy eatery that the few staff members on duty thought no one would be coming in before they closed up early in the face of a snowstorm that the weather service warned had Armonk in its crosshairs.

As I entered the stone-silent restaurant, I felt as if the staff was going to tell me that lunch was done for the day. I could hear it loud and clear before anyone said a word: "Thanks but no thanks. See you next time."

But their response was diametrically opposite. Quickly, the young food staff, all in their twenties, snapped into action, turning up the thermostat, offering me a complimentary cup of hot coffee, and taking my order.

I was the only patron in the place and from all indications, it would likely stay that way, but this team was determined to see to it that I was happily ensconced in the warm environment they created for me. I had a wonderful meal of soup and turkey, ordered a mini feast to take home with me, and left the chef and the waitress $50 each. I don't throw money around, but I do acknowledge excellence and being treated like a family member on a night when the boss was gone and the weather was miserable—I just loved the unexpected hospitality and I knew that the person in charge (who was likely in Barbados himself) understood how to create a winning culture and why it is so crucial to building and growing an exceptional business.

Now ask yourself, how does your team behave when you are not looking? Would they have turned me away or treated me as if I was a guest in their own kitchen?

Great cultures, the kind that drive profitable and growing companies, exhibit the following characteristics:

1. They view the "gold standard" as inadequate. If you can aspire to platinum, the thinking goes, why settle for gold? (In companies that suck, bronze, copper—anything—is deemed just fine.)

2. The employees don't have jobs; they have signed up for a mission. It's a U.S. Marine Corps-type culture that views success as the only possible outcome. From my perspective, the dazzling companies—the ones that know how to consistently thrill their clients and customers—function as a fusion of chess players and Marines: instead of simply going through the motions, they develop an ingenious strategy and then execute it like a driven, nonstop force.

3. They are on a journey of constant self-improvement. This refusal to accept the current state of service or quality as good enough is the driver of all great cultures, whether it is a company of two people or 20,000. This determination to succeed

beyond normal expectations always pays major dividends. It stems from the leader's commitment and ability to:

- Establish a thrilling goal.
- Demonstrate how everyone can play an important role in achieving it.
- Work harder than anyone else and be willing to help employees at any level in the company when their plates are full or their energy wanes. (They are like great generals, who march ahead of their troops rather than issuing commands from safe havens.)
- Make certain that the wealth of the company is shared by all who help to generate it.
- Fire those who do not. Cancer destroys companies faster than it kills people.

Forward-Moving vs. Stagnant Companies

Companies with restless, achievement-focused cultures succeed in any economy or competitive scenario. Examine a highly successful company, one that thrives over time, and you will recognize that in addition to its patents, trademarks, and exceptional people, it is driven forward by a proud and relentless culture.

When a business suffers instead from a destructive, cannibalistic culture, the fault lies not with the employees but with the leader who has failed to lead. This always takes a heavy toll on the business.

Here is a case in point. Immediately before 9/11, I met with a prospective client in Dallas. The president and owner of a consumer products manufacturing company had asked me to fly out, tour his plant, and discuss a possible business relationship.

Once a robust enterprise with what seemed to be a the-sky's-the-limit future, the company had been riddled over the years by a chain reaction of setbacks, including cheap foreign imports and the rise of a savvy class of online competitors. By the time we met, the company's revenues had fallen 42 percent from its peak, profits had vanished, and the future had gloom and doom written all over it.

On the surface, it seemed like a natural set of disasters had befallen the company. But that wasn't really true. The truth behind its imminent demise lay in a conversation the president and I had about his unions.

> PRESIDENT: We're a union shop. Two-thirds of our employees are organized.
>
> MS: That has to make the situation even more difficult to address.
>
> PRESIDENT: Not really. We get along very well with our unions. In fact, there's no tension at all, and we're quite proud of that.

I was engaged to help turn the company around, and began the process of discovery, which is always a critical first step. It didn't take me long to put the union issue in perspective. The cordial relationship with the local was due not to its willingness to make deep concessions to a troubled company (and in fact it was not willing to do so) but instead to the passive culture that was the company's unfortunate hallmark. The president challenged no one, sought to please everyone, and overall presided (if you can call it that) over an entity that blew in the wind rather than collecting itself, revising its founding strategy, moving production offshore, and building a strong e-commerce business.

It was, before I came on the scene and forced holistic change, a culture of acceptance, of neglect, of "hope springs eternal." The company sucked on every front, but in spite of this, the owner saw himself as a victim as opposed to the blind and benign culprit that he was. In this case—emblematic of so many others—a passive and entitled culture was the enemy within.

3.

Declare War on Complacency and Incompetence

A company can devolve from a standard of performance that is exceptional or even simply acceptable to the point at which it fails to achieve on virtually any level pretty much anywhere in its lifecycle: at the outset, in midcourse, or in the later stages of its evolution.

The key point is that the mere passage of time does not cause the erosion of pride, excellence, functionality, or superiority. Instead, the culprit is the onset of dysfunctionality. Strategic and tactical gaps, complacency, oversight, nearsightedness, neglect, small thinking, and a host of other flaws tear at the fabric and the spirit of a business, leading it down the primrose path to mediocrity or worse.

The fact that time alone is *not* the issue—that companies are not doomed to start off on wobbly legs or to move through the years to a fatalistic meeting with a sorry and broken business model—is a good thing. Why? Because just as your business is not locked into a time warp that will hold it hostage to its own failings, neither is it ever too early or too late to transition your business from sucking to soaring.

This is not a Pollyannaish pipe dream. Just as you, as a private person, can always change something about yourself at any time—lose weight, learn another language, sever a relationship gone awry—so, too, can you make the decision to turn around and revive a sloppy, dull, or defective business at any time.

To do so, you must declare war. Once a company has become dysfunctional and twisted, there is no magic wand to solve its problems. The people and practices that led to subpar performance seep into the nooks and crannies of the business, and like a stain on a reputation, are difficult to remove. Worse yet, the bureaucracy (which can start to take hold of an organization with just a handful of people) resists change (whether it is for the better or not), viewing it as a threat to the status quo, which it understands, is comfortable in, and, perverted as it may be, adores. The irrefutable fact is that once a company reaches a point that it disappoints more than

> *The irrefutable fact is that once a company reaches a point that it disappoints more than it thrills (if it thrills at all), driving a true turnaround is daunting.*

it thrills (if it thrills at all), driving a true turnaround is daunting.

Quality Matters

This brings us to the need to issue a declaration of war on your business—constructive war, to be sure, but war nevertheless. To wage this war successfully—and to propel the company to soar again (or for the first time)—you will have to declare war on the quality of your products and services. Yes, they may be good, but good is not good enough.

We don't thrive in business by avoiding complaints. We do so by thrilling the pants off of the people we are privileged to serve.

Think of the difference you experience, even savor, when a hotel you frequent upgrades its interior, adds flat screens and Wi-Fi, and opens a dazzling new restaurant. Even if you were content with the lodging before, the upgrade makes you fall in love all over again. You will seek excuses to return more often, you will serve as a viral advocate for the hotel, which, by raising the bar on its own level of quality, will have placed a firewall around you and other hoteliers competing for your business.

Are you thinking, "Oh, that's not me. My company's quality level is already off the charts with little room for improvement"? Be aware that this form of complacency is, indeed, a slippery slope. No matter how high you rank on the quality hierarchy, you simply cannot be content with the quality standard you have in place, even if you haven't had a single complaint or other reason to challenge it. We don't thrive in business by avoiding complaints. We do so by thrilling the pants off of the people we are privileged to serve. And we do this in great measure by racing far ahead of our customers' expectations.

Attracting New Customers While Still Thrilling the Old Ones

For a business to be dynamic, to drive growth, the company must continuously identify and capture new customers. When all is functioning properly, the sales process is the catalyst for filling the pipeline with leads and converting them into new sources of revenues.

For the genuine hunters (those with the rare ability to identify and cultivate new opportunities), this process is thrilling. Securing a lead and then transforming that opportunity into a monetized reality is one of the magical acts of business. Every time you pull off this feat, you'll feel a pure adrenaline rush.

I like to think of it as analogous to the classic *Superman* episode in which the Man of Steel squeezes a lump of coal into a diamond. Anyone who has ever made a sale from scratch knows it is a thing of beauty.

However, it's all too easy to forget an important caveat in the euphoria of the moment. Sorry to rain on your parade, but I've seen what can go wrong too many times to ignore it; soon after the sale has been made, the champagne glasses have been raised, and the bubbles have evaporated, the *lust* for the onetime prospect (now a customer) turns to *lax*. What do I mean by this? Almost instantly, the former object of desire is dumped into the customer database and, in the vast majority of cases, taken for granted. The lust that drives the sales machine turns to the next prospect and the customer is left behind.

Let me drive this point home. Over a six-year period, I purchased two Porsche Targas. In each case, I was torn between the Porsche and a Mercedes SL 500. The salespeople at the dealerships competed for my business at every turn, calling frequently, sweetening the offers, promising to throw in every kind of tempting accessory at no charge.

The former object of desire is dumped into the customer database and, in the vast majority of cases, taken for granted. The lust that drives the sales machine turns to the next prospect and the customer is left behind.

Each time I chose the Porsche, I picked up my shiny new toy, drove away, and never heard a word from the dealer/salesperson again until I returned three years later to consider another purchase.

What was going on here is an all-too-common syndrome; the moment that I wrote my check, the Porsche guys transitioned me from an object of lust to a number in a database, a digital code on a server. The salesperson was off to find the next customer, lusting after the next prospect while I was dumped into the "conquered him" file. (I finally switched to a Mercedes SL.)

This takes us into the heart of why so many companies fail to thrill, and why, in turn, they consistently underperform; they lapse into the lust-to-lax syndrome that turns off the very people they want to serve as loyal customers and viral advocates of their businesses. The dysfunctional process moves in this distorted direction:

1. We lust after prospects.
2. We treat them indifferently once they become customers.
3. We move immediately to transition new prospects into customers without putting a system in place to ensure that the people already among our most precious assets (our customers) are and remain thrilled with our people, products, and services.

The key to creating a sustainable and scalable business is to treat the customer as the royalty of the business—the men and women lavished with the best of everything:

- Unique offers
- Exceptional service
- Unforgettable experiences
- Family member status

The best way to ensure that your company pays attention to the details, the finer points of a business relationship, is to appoint a Chief Customer Officer who has the power to make certain that every one of the company's strategies and tactics is designed with the customer in mind. Today, your customers are likely little more than names on a server. Tomorrow, they must be members of an exclusive club.

We all see the failure of other companies to do this: the bank that treats us as a number, the hotel we visit every year that never remembers the room we adore, the auto dealer who counts us as among the dead between purchases—but we refuse to see it in our own businesses. And that's a major reason your company may suck!

> *Appoint a Chief Customer Officer who has the power to make certain that every one of the company's strategies and tactics is designed with the customer in mind.*

Go for Meritocracy, Fight Tenor-Track Mode

What system do you have in place (or more telling, do you have one?) for rewarding and promoting employees?

My thoughts on how you should organize your incentives may surprise you because, like much of my thinking, they run contrary to conventional wisdom. Here's a case in point: conventional thinking holds that it is typical for employers to treat their employees with disrespect, but my experience is the polar opposite of this. The proverbial big bad boss is much more uncommon (and thus much less of a problem—I rarely see it) than the pushover teddy bear boss.

Look behind the stereotypes and you'll find that the all-too-common scenario is to promote and reward employees on the basis of tenure as opposed to performance.

Every year, usually in the glow of the holiday season, employees are rewarded with a raise, say 7 percent, often across the board, with little or no correlation with performance. The knee-jerk response is, "You are here, you can fog a mirror, you get a raise."

Although this seems generous at first blush, think of the encrypted message this policy sends to the workforce: everyone deserves the same salary even though some of you work much harder and smarter than the others. Between the lines, the company is signaling that it does not recognize and reinforce excellence, drive, determination, achievement, or loyalty. Regardless of where you fall on the performance curve—in spite of your contribution to the company or lack of it—you are paid based on the same compensation structure as your peers.

Management is tone-deaf and, even worse, operating under the dangerous illusion that it can apply the principles of a socialistic entitlement state to a free-market enterprise. This amounts to electioneering, as if the manager were seeking to win a popularity contest rather than tossing out all of the politically correct nonsense in favor of a fierce determination to build and motivate the best possible performers and shape them into an extraordinary team.

In the vacuum created by this populist management approach (designed to keep the peace by bending over backwards to make certain that no group of employees is made to feel left behind in terms of compensation and titles), a culture of tenure takes hold. But here's the rub: you don't get tenure in the real world.

Tenure is a stake in the heart of private enterprise. As much as the Harvard faculty might protest, *tenure* is a euphemism. It is an intellectual way of camouflaging the truth by saying that you can stay on the job, protected by the rules, even if your performance is as original and captivating as Muzak.

Unfortunately, teddy bear leaders too often put their companies' futures in the hands of tenured slackers. Normally, natural evolutionary forces of the marketplace would weed out these underperforming employees, but they are protected by their leaders' hesitance to disturb the culture of tenure.

> *Tenure is a euphemism. It is an intellectual way of camouflaging the truth by saying that you can stay on the job, protected by the rules, even if your performance is as original and captivating as Muzak.*

When my sons were youngsters and occasionally under the thumb of dreadful teachers who were lazy, incompetent, arrogant—and, from all I could judge, were simply going through the motions at my children's expense—I would press a case at the Grafflin School in Chappaqua, New York, only to find that *right* and *wrong* had no place in the lexicon of tenure. The school principal (where my hearings usually wound up) turned out to be a glorified shop steward who had determined, before he heard a word of my thinking, that I was wrong and the teachers were right. It didn't matter what they did or didn't do—the verdict was in, case closed, the teachers were innocent of all charges, whatever they might be.

This is tenure in action; it destroys companies much as it has ravaged once-great academic institutions.

More recently, I have tried to alert U.S. national security officials of terror threats that one of my firm's clients—Safe Banking Systems—is uniquely capable of detecting. But as a *New York Times* reporter working the case with me has pointed out, "Bureaucrats don't want to know that others may know more than them." Why should they bother, given that they get paid regardless of outcome?

Companies large and small are saddled with parasite employees who spend much of their time smoking, lunching, taking coffee breaks, and bitching about everything under the sun. They keep their place because of unions who don't know how to spell the word *performance*.

Every time I meet a company for the first time, and management brags to me that no one in the organization has been fired for 30 years or so, I know tenure is written on the walls and that third-rate hangers-on soak up the payroll and sap the company of its vitality. Tenure rather than meritocracy is the driving force there.

The truth is, except for the U.S. Supreme Court, there is no place for tenure. People, ideas, products, services, strategies—all must earn their place in the real-world markets or be swept away by the meritocracy established and upheld by the leader, the president, the CEO. The question is, how do you establish and maintain this high-performance environment?

The Seven Commandments of a Meritocracy-Driven Business

In a well-run company, raises and promotions should be based on measurable performance:

1. You bring in profitable business.
2. You grow existing business organically.
3. You promote the company's mission.
4. You give *more* than your job profile demands of you.
5. You are a cheerleader for the company.
6. You bring new ideas to the table.
7. You are a true collaborator.

In effect, employees are expected (make that *required*) to raise the exponent over the company's name and its performance, to make it greater than the sum of its parts.

Declaring war requires management to make it abundantly clear to all employees that they must achieve this high standard—that there is no such thing as a great company with slacker employees—or find work elsewhere. This cannot be accomplished through a series of threats. The only action that works (because it protects your credibility and fires a shot across the bow) is to:

1. Encourage and reward the winners.
2. Discuss the ways you want those with low grades to raise the bar. Talk to them. Mentor them.

3. Warn those who fail to heed your message.
4. Enforce accountability throughout the ranks.
5. Terminate those who think you are bluffing.

Unconventional Thinking in Music and Heroes

I watched an interview with Van Morrison on an episode of *CBS Sunday Morning*. Here is a singer/songwriter who has had a thriving career for a generation and a half, who has gained admission to the Rock and Roll Hall of Fame, and who was personally inducted into The Song Writers Hall Of Fame by Ray Charles.

But most of all, Morrison has been an entertainer who has complete disdain for the *book of entertainment*. He is an introvert. He does not connect with his audiences. He feels it is more important to connect with his mind and his soul, even when thousands of fans are clapping their hands in the rows and rows of seats before him. He refused to attend his own induction to the Rock and Roll Hall of Fame. He dislikes everything about fame except that it drives people to listen to his music.

There is zero spin in the man. The interview on CBS is painful. But he has made, and continues to make, extraordinary music. That is *his book*. That is his rule. If he worried about the star power machinery that comes with every record contract, chances are good the music would have gone silent years ago.

If you live life by the book, you cut off the potential to learn the wonders and powers that we can stumble upon if we are open to adventure and discovery. No matter who we are or the extent of our education, there is far more we don't know than what we do. We sit on top of the iceberg, often proud of our level of knowledge or expertise, and are blind to all that is above and below us.

This Great Recession is a crisis, of course, but also proof positive of how little we actually know. The allegedly best and brightest among us in finance and economics have no idea how to get us out of the problem they caused. Why? Because they are doing it by the book—looking to Keynes, pursuing Adam Smith, studying FDR. But those guys didn't read the books, they wrote them.

From among the rubble of the GMs and the GEs of this 1929 redux (or close to it or worse than it) will come a new generation of American heroes. They'll be virtual book shunners—men and women who reject conventional knowledge, blaze new paths, find new solutions, and in the process create accidental businesses and become random millionaires.

4.

Where Are You in the Business Lifecycle?

O ne of the key goals of this book is to identify—
and then act on—the red flags warning you
that your company or business unit is broken
before the issues at the core of its dysfunction become
life threatening. While knowing which of the four reasons a company might be failing—rudderless leadership,
complacency resulting from the lust-to-lax syndrome,
incompetence, and using conventional thinking rather
than thinking outside the box to thrill (more on that
later)—is affecting your business, it's also important to
know what phase of business your company is in.

Virtually all companies move through a similar business lifecycle to varying degrees—and the hope is to
avoid phases four and five. The cycle is rife with issues,
challenges, and opportunities that must be addressed as
the business evolves.

The Five Phases of the Business Lifecycle

Where are you in the cycle?

1. Infancy.

Phase 1 Traits
• Exploratory stage • Establish identity • Develop code breaker • Implement structure

The company is formed and grows slowly. It is finding its sea legs, testing messages, experimenting with product selections, and deciding on the proper array of products and services to offer in the marketplace. Consider this an exploratory stage where the initial idea for the business meets the reality of structuring it and facing the unforgiving and, if you are open to it, extraordinarily valuable feedback of the marketplace.

Of course, there are exceptions, but as a rule, this nascent stage is not marked by a skyrocketing trajectory. The wise business owner uses the early stage to carefully observe how the business is playing out, as founding ideas and concepts are transitioned to pragmatic application. The goal is to develop what I call a *code breaker*—that combination of product/service, pricing, and marketing that lights a fire under sales and leads to scalable and sustainable growth.

When I first launched my current company, MSCO, I focused on charging for so-called marketing deliverables—brochures, newsletters, direct response mailers, print advertisements, and the like—and threw in my strategic thinking capabilities for free. It seemed to me to be the best way to offer a high-value service that my competitors could not match.

It was. But there wasn't a single good reason not to charge fees for the substantial business insights I was delivering. So in this early stage of the business, I hit upon the code breaker for my company: focusing on being one of the few marketing firms capable of developing business growth strategies, leading with this, making this the key driver of revenue, and moving the deliverables to the back of the supply/value chain.

FRIENDSHIP AND BUSINESS LIKE A BAD MIXED DRINK

Phase 1 of the business lifecycle seems great, a time of new beginnings, clean slates, a company brimming with possibility. But all is not what it seems. Ironically, the seeds of problems that will come to plague the business in the future are often planted in the slow-growth early years.

This is particularly prevalent when friends launch the venture as a partnership. This sounds like a marriage made in heaven because the partners like and complement each other. But the truth is, the friendship often leads to agreement on issues for the sake of camaraderie as opposed to standing one's ground or even engaging in conflict—a good thing when this internal debate is important for the business.

> *The seeds of problems that will come to plague the business in the future are often planted in the slow-growth early years.*

Additionally, the lines of authority between the friends are not clearly delineated and, as others come into the company, they, too, are caught up in the fuzzy logic that becomes the foundation of the company's culture. It can all feel warm and clubby in the nascent stages, but this turns to chaos as the enterprise adds people and complexity to the mix.

I worked with a hair-products manufacturing company launched by some Syracuse University grads who were onetime sorority sisters and fancied themselves as tighter than blood sisters. In terms of friendship they may have been close, but business and friendship are hardly one and the same. They didn't understand the distinction. To their way of thinking, running the business as if they were still cruising around campus in the coed years would be the secret sauce for an extraordinary company, the winning recipe to set them apart from the competition.

At first, the spirit of *kumbaya* worked like a charm. There was a warmth to the enterprise, a sense of belonging, and a quasi-family ethos that left everyone feeling like they were owners. This is nice in theory but horrific in practice. Why? Because what started out so peachy didn't stay that way. Fast-forward to 2011, ten years after the company's formation. How is this for a friendship gone awry?

First, the salesperson covering the company's most important territory—New York's boroughs of Manhattan, Brooklyn, and Queens—lives in Stockholm. Yes, as in Sweden. When Patricia's husband was relocated to that charming Scandinavian city, Pat naturally wanted to go with him... without giving up her job at the hair products company and without parting ways with her "sisters." And so they all agreed that she could maintain her New York sales territory, move to Sweden, never see a customer again, and collect her salary in full. She would call the salons once a month, taking the orders she could get, and call it a win/win. (Yes, sometimes truth really is stranger than fiction.)

Second, when customers made it clear that they wanted new products to complement the existing line, the founders sent out the word to the most innovative sisters, those charged with developing new products, to come up with the winners that would blow away the customer base and the competition.

The response? Zero! No one even bothered to get back to the founders. Why? They were sisters and, unlike in a corporate structure, where employees *must* answer and respond to the boss, sisters can choose to ignore each other—which is precisely what they did. Case closed.

---

2. *Accelerated Growth.*

Phase 2 Traits

- Growth begins
- Solid leadership guides the company
- Disciplined environment exists

Management does something or many things well, and the business takes off and grows rapidly.

Consider this the by-product of the experimentation and testing done in Phase 1. As the business gains more structure and begins to identify its best skills, as well as home in on its sweet spots in the marketplace, growth accelerates markedly.

Admin Server was once a small tech startup in the financial services space, founded by two software pros with a game-changing idea for bringing new products to market far faster and less expensively than traditional means allowed. This would be a boon to every company engaged in the development of insurance, annuities, and investment instruments, as the first to market often commanded the highest share of sales for years.

When my friend Rick Connors's firm, The MONY Group, was acquired by AXA, Connors earned a handsome payout and decided to transition from the executive suite (where he ran MONY's annuities business) to an entrepreneurial venture. Connors, who had installed the then-fledgling Admin Server's product when he'd worked at MONY, decided to join Admin Server as president. With Rick's management and leadership skills, he was able to give the company the structure and discipline it needed to rocket past the start-up stage, to expand more than tenfold in two years; soon thereafter, it was acquired by Oracle.

In short, Connors was able to whip a smart but ragtag organization into a selling machine that experienced dramatic growth and quickly commanded a substantial market share.

3. Leveling Out.

Phase 3 Traits

- Growth stops
- Complacency is a danger
- Management is not adapting to change
- There's still time to turn it around

The high-growth period runs its course and the business plateaus. What does the plateau stage look like? Here are the signs:

- **Revenues have either leveled off, are declining slightly, or the pace of growth has slowed markedly.** In many cases, the latter is the most dangerous. Why? Because the company is still growing (albeit at a more modest pace), so it is easy to overlook the problems that may be looming over the business. But look you must: there is a reason the pace has slowed considerably.

- **Customer complaints are on the rise.** It's nothing like a full-scale revolt, but for the first time, you are hearing a rumbling of discontent. The temptation is to address the complaints as isolated incidents, but once the drumbeat becomes steady, the plateau—and likely worse—is just over the horizon.

- **Employees are seeking raises in greater numbers than usual.** It may, in fact, seem that everyone wants a raise at the same time. Of course, people always want to earn more, but as a company begins to decline or settle into a plateau period, the culture suffers, and the sense of excitement that comes with being part of a mission begins to deteriorate. In this environment, where the intangibles lose their value, the chorus of voices seeking raises expands dramatically.

People always want to earn more, but as a company begins to decline or settle into a plateau period, the culture suffers and the sense of excitement that comes with being part of a mission begins to deteriorate. In this environment, where the intangibles lose their value, the chorus of voices seeking raises expands dramatically.

Think of it this way: no one serving passengers on Southwest flights makes big money but virtually all are proud and happy to be part of the best team in the air.

The day that changes—that flying Southwest is the same miserable experience as suffering on Continental or United—management needs to read these tea leaves as the signs of a plateau.

The great thing about a company at a plateau is that it has not yet taken a nosedive into the disaster zone. The plateau stage is salvageable, and it's where my company often comes in to do damage control and retool things.

My goal at MSCO is to take hold of the runaway business and begin to engineer a turnaround, well before the free-fall period, ideally at the plateau stage. A business entering or already in the plateau stage of its lifecycle emits a set of signals that—if you are vigilant and willing to read the writing on the wall and accept it for the bad omen it is—can help you respond before conditions deteriorate.

It helps to understand how you got to the plateau in the first place. Typically, the plateau occurs because the business does one or more of the following:

- **Fails to refresh its offerings.** The hot products or services that launched the business and provided its initial thrust have lost their appeal. For example, there was an eyeglasses chain of five stores that hit a major code breaker with a punky/hip-hop look that appealed to young people (and those not so young but determined to retain the illusion of youth); it rode the crest of the wave for three years, opening new stores at a rapid clip. But the fashion wheel always turns, often quickly and unexpectedly, and when it did, the chain found itself saddled with an image, inventory, and a myopic management mindset that was hurting the business, locked as it was in the straits of yesterday's look.

- **Lacks resilient managers.** Management is often a cause of a business's plateau issue rather than being part of the cure. That is because managers/owners tend to dig in during times of stress, believing (when the tide begins to turn) they are in a battle with customers as opposed to being in a form of partnership. Wise businesspeople recognize that they are not in a war of wills with their clients/customers; instead they're locked in a battle to stay ahead of the inevitable curve that brings new styles, products, services, offers, pricing systems, and the like to the marketplace. When management is driven to resist rather than revise, the company plateaus.

- **Suffers from complacent managers.** Management also can fall into the complacency trap, believing that a company's rapid growth period implies a lifelong guarantee of continuous, high-octane increases in sales and revenues. This is why early success can be a blessing and a curse. To prevent this entitlement mentality, and, in

turn, the plateau that comes with it, management must wake up every day determined to be, as Michael Dell has said, "the
biggest start-up in the business." Expect
nothing, but fight for everything.

4. Slow Death.

Phase 4 Traits

- Slow death begins
- Management walks around in a haze
- "Hope springs eternal" employees fail to
  face reality

The company begins to go out of business slowly. Management, confused and disoriented like a pilot in fog, has
failed to deal effectively with the flattening company trajectory that occurred in Phase 3. Accordingly, the company begins to shrink.

The telltale signs include:

- Declining sales that can no longer be dismissed as an aberation. The downward
  direction is clear and appears to be un-
  stoppable.

- The best team members flee, leaving the company to join competitors or to become competitors in their own right.
- Customers vent their anxiety that something appears wrong with the company—and they actually worry about engaging in long-term contracts with it.

It happens so gradually that the first signs of possible demise go undetected by you or your managers (who are in denial or so irrationally optimistic that they believe—with zero evidence to support this—that "next year will be better. Next year will be better. Next year will be better...").

There is both good news and bad news in this fourth phase of a business. The most dangerous part of the corporate lifecycle is the very point when the company begins to go out of business slowly—but it's also the point where the process is the most reversible. So if you're at this point, it's not too late to turn the tide. The key is to recognize the plateau, not wait until you're free-falling.

The most dangerous part of the corporate lifecycle is the very point when the company begins to go out of business slowly—but it's also the point where the process is the most reversible. So if you're at this point, it's not too late to turn the tide. The key is to recognize the plateau, not wait until you're free-falling.

5. *Major Free Fall: RIP.*

Phase 5 Traits

- Company burial is imminent
- There is a controlled state of panic
- Employee morale has tanked
- Leaders are angry
- Loyal customers are being punished

The company begins to go out of business rapidly, often in free fall. The end is near. This last phase is usually marked by a state of chaos:

- The boss is mad but doesn't quite know who to vent her anger at.
- Customers who have remained loyal to the bitter end are *rewarded* with harsher credit terms and deteriorating products and services.
- Employee morale, already on the ropes for some time, turns to outright bitterness followed by a rush to the exit doors.
- The place is a virtual disaster zone.
- Cash flow is negative, inventory is sparse, and employee count has dipped below the

point that customers can be well served by even the most modest standards.

- In a typical day, everyone is spending 90 percent of the time trying to put out fires—and for every blaze that is extinguised another takes its place.

SOMETIMES IT'S JUST TOO LATE

In its heyday, one of our clients was *the* leader in its industry. The entrepreneur who founded the business turned a brainstorm into a startup that brought a dynamic sales methodology to a market that had been dominated by sleepy players, all conforming to a tired business model.

Initially, advertisers—who would purchase their media time through the new venture—were slow to adopt the new approach. But as the first movers gravitated toward the service and raved about it, others followed suit; within two years, the company

Within two years, the company entered an explosive growth phase that would take the founders on a magic carpet ride that would last for decades. Euphoria, matched by a sense of entitlement and permanence, set in.

entered an explosive growth phase that would take the founders on a magic carpet ride that would last for

decades. Euphoria, matched by a sense of entitlement and permanence, set in.

"For a while, our biggest problem was keeping
clear of the big glass windows that lined our Madi-
son Avenue offices," the founder reminisced. "So
much money was blowing into the place at such a
fast and furious velocity that we didn't want to get
knocked down by it."

The business was innovative, passionate, and wildly profitable, driven by a management corps and a
sales team that was on fire. When the company went
public, everyone got rich . . . on paper.

And then two forces converged to reshape the
business:

- A recession struck, plunging a knife into ad
  sales.

- Complacency took hold. The management
  team that had been able to coast for years
  lost its fighting spirit and allowed the
  marketplace to drive its fate rather than
  fighting back by developing strategies and
  promotions that would rekindle the flame.

For the first time, the company suffered a losing
year. And then another and another. The losses, at
this point at least, were minor—but the reversal of
fortune and the loss of momentum were catastrophic.

The biggest problem was that no one saw it this
way. Instead, consensus inside the company was that
the economy was to blame and that a rebounding
economy would be the catalyst for a turnaround. As

the prevailing Pollyannaish mindset viewed it, once macroeconomics did its magic, the company would be returned to its high-flying ways by the jet stream, taking with it the company's stock price, which reached $42 at its zenith.

This "Oh, it'll get better" (aka "hope springs eternal") mentality blinded management to the hard, cold fact that this business was on the skids, in the very early stages of "going out of business slowly."

By the time my firm was called in to help rescue the business, the free fall was wreaking havoc throughout the crumbling enterprise. Sales were nose-diving, clients were in open revolt, accounts were being lost every week, and the stock price had collapsed to less than a dollar.

This was a company going out of business quickly. This was a business with zero sense of magic. This was a business that was hard to do business with. Customers were breaking contracts at the risk of legal retaliation just to free themselves of the misery, the sloppiness, and the arrogance of working with the firm.

This "Oh, it'll get better" (aka "hope springs eternal") mentality—which grips so many companies—blinded management to the hard, cold fact that this business was on the skids, in the very early stages of "going out of business slowly."

At our first meeting, the founder volunteered, "We don't suck...I wish I could say that. We totally, miserably, awfully suck. We suck...squared."

He tried to present a sense of bravado, that this was a firm that would rebound, but I saw *it* in his

eyes. The panic. The depression. The exasperation...
the Look. There was no longer a question if they had
a severe problem. As is true with so many of these
sloppy scenarios, the question was what to do next.

Although MSCO swung into action to turn the
business around, management had waited too long,
allowing the business to deteriorate so badly that events
were now beyond our control. Just as we were getting
started, vulture investors began to circle the company,
buying up stock and debt for pennies on the dollar. Soon,
these bottom feeders would force the issue, taking over
the company and leaving the founder with a tiny fraction of the wealth he had accumulated just a few years before.

At our first meeting, the founder volunteered, "We don't suck... I wish I could say that. We totally, miserably, awfully suck. We suck... squared."

A once-great business, a money machine, had
slipped away precisely because it didn't understand
the lifecycle warning signs, and it stopped thrilling
its customers in every way.

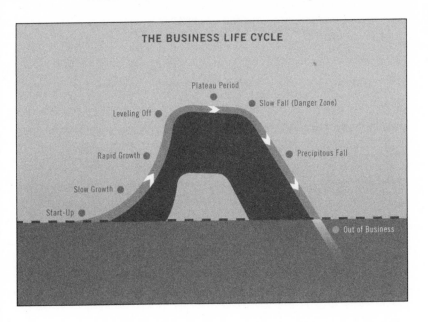

5.

You Don't Have to Stay Where You Are

If you've plateaued or even if you're skyrocketing down-ward, you don't have to continue on that trajectory. Let's look at how three companies turned things around.

IBM

When a company doesn't adapt to the new culture and market, it loses its upward trajectory. IBM is a case in point. As the world was moving *en masse* to PC technol-ogy, IBM was clinging stubbornly to the mainframe. The company's plateau period of the late 1980s turned into an Amazon of red ink in the early 1990s.

As advisors to a number of IBM business units, my firm and I watched the downfall from courtside box seats—we saw the chaos unfold at IBM before the cavalry (in the form of Lou Gerstner) was called in to take the helm from John Akers. Whether a company is large like IBM or small or midsized, the patterns that bring down once-fine companies are often similar in enterprises ranging from the Fortune 500 to a neighborhood furniture store. And what we witnessed at Big Blue is typical for companies in their death throes. Some signs might be:

- No one will make a decision on anything. I used to say, in only a mild exaggeration, that it takes two hours to decide where to have lunch.

- Everyone is covering their butts, refusing to sign documents, agreements, vendor invoices, etc.—no one wants their fingerprints anywhere near the scene of the crime.

- The entire team, from top to bottom, appears to have given up. Silence and inaction reign as all gather around to watch the *Titanic* sink, with no one even trying to right the ship.

- No one seems to be working, so the place is graveyard quiet. There are no debates, discussions, presentations, or brainstorming sessions. The patient's vital signs appear ready to shut down. Just when the business needs a champion, there isn't a hard worker to be found. Anyone still at his desk after 4:30 is having an affair with a co-worker or playing video games.

A mass exodus might be next. In the last days of Vietnam, I recall Americans leaving Saigon. Everyone wanted out. There were thousands waiting for the last copter out of the U.S. Embassy. That's much like the scene I have witnessed at so many companies that are succumbing to the plague, to their sins of commission and omission, and that are at death's door.

Interestingly, as I have noted, that last stage of the life cycle does not have to occur. The company, regardless of its condition, can stage a comeback. Gerstner did just that by:

- Adapting to a changing market and morphing IBM into a major services provider.
- Not caring a whit about the lack of popularity he was generating among the old hands who had brought the business to the brink.
- Developing a clear new vision and executing it with precision.
- Personally visiting with the company's customers to take their heat openly and then gathering their input on how IBM could once again reign over the corporate landscape as a valued business partner.

Is IBM an isolated case? Are there other times when it is too late to save a troubled business by engineering a turnaround? The answer is almost always *no, it's never too late*. Providing you have the will, the drive, the guts, and the *I will do anything to save and then revive this business* mindset, you can truly turn it around.

This is true because most companies sliding on a downward trajectory are not selling a product or services that are no longer in demand. Something has happened to the company's culture, process, leadership, or any combination of these elements (as I have outlined for you), and any or all of these can be addressed.

Here are two more cases in point, first a large company and then a small business.

Apple Bites

After Steve Jobs was unceremoniously and embarrassingly fired from Apple, the company he co-founded, the once high-flying business was written off as dead. For years, the experts predicted that Mac technology—a relic of the past, the loser in the early and most famous competition of the Information Age—would be completely washed away in the mounting tsunami of Microsoft's operating system.

According to many highly credentialed technologists holding court everywhere from MIT to the Gartner Group, Apple was doomed—a lovable curio of the industry's infancy but not long for this world.

Steve Jobs's view was the polar opposite. Surely, he recognized—more than anyone else did or cared to because it was his baby they were ruining—that Apple was a basket case of a company. He saw all of the telltale signs in damaged leadership, innovation, reputation, and morale.

But he knew that even a company in free fall can be turned around. Once he returned to the helm, he did just that by focusing on a simple but powerful model that was embedded in the company from the start: Innovate + Execute + Innovate.

This I+E+I model has led to:

- iTunes
- iPhone
- iPad

Apple's virtual reinvention of the music and video distribution system led to an extraordinary resurgence in Mac technology. This all culminated in Apple, the company, surpassing Microsoft in total value, known as market capitalization.

David not only beat the odds, he ate Goliath for lunch.

Weather Patterns

On a small-business level, a small New Jersey-based HVAC company, AirFlow Systems, saw its revenues begin to decline steadily, an ugly by-product of a sluggish economy and the even more troubling fact that management had never developed anything to set the company apart from the competition. As such, it was a commodity player lacking any weapons to fight for market share in a declining space.

What to do? Hope for a change in the economy? That's not exactly a management strategy. No, the key would be to develop a positioning, a branding, and a marketing campaign to support it that would separate and distinguish AirFlow Systems from the other commodity players in the marketplace. This would provide the company with the firepower to claim a far higher share of the HVAC space and empower it with a platform for reversing course and taking the market by storm.

In order to accomplish this, MSCO, which led the turnaround, had to take a set of challenging and decisive steps, including:

- Changing the company's name to The Weather Busters (how's that for a 180-degree turn from AirFlow Systems?).
- Developing proactive branding for The Weather Busters.
- Redesigning all of the trucks, uniforms, signage, and many of the sales processes.
- Launching a major radio advertising campaign built around the 24/7 The Weather Busters theme.

Was it too late for the company to reverse engines and soar back to the top? Never! In fact, the new approach is a prototype for taking what was once a local business national through the power of franchising.

6.

An Action Plan for Change

Human redemption is one of the great things in life. We can go wildly off the rails and work to redeem ourselves. The same is true for every business in the world. The question is, if your company sucks, when will you act to redeem it, to turn it around? How about now?

Timing isn't the issue. Methodology is. What can you do when you see that your company has reached that dangerous plateau? What do you do when you look in the mirror and see that sign of fear in your eyes?

If you are in Phase 4 or 5, you need to move expeditiously to adopt an action plan. One that will be effective enough to turn your company around must not only sniff out and correct any of the four reasons that your business has suffered—rudderless leadership, the lust-to-lax

syndrome, incompetence, and conventional thinking—
but must also focus on how to get (and keep) customers
hooked on your business. You don't want your customers happy, you want them *thrilled*. The following is my
four-step Action Plan.

Step 1: View Your Business with Fresh Eyes

Where do you fail to exceed the norm for quality and
service in your industry? In which facets of your business do you accept conventional levels of customer satisfaction as good enough? (Hint: You shouldn't, because
it never is!)

Make a list of each and every aspect of your mediocrity. Granted, this may be difficult because a) we get
married to the ways we do business, good, bad, or indif-
ferent, and instinctively we want to defend and protect
the status quo; b) we can become blind to or short-sighted
about our own failures; and c) we may not be aware of
superior options.

To see through your business with a powerful new
prism, conduct a *Discovery*, a process designed to identify every way your business falls short of excellence—of
the ability to thrill customers, earning their loyalty and
their viral advocacy. The Discovery process serves as a
compass for turning around a business on the skids and/
or identifying incipient problems before they can wreak
havoc on the business.

The process can be accomplished, in part, by:

- Asking trusted peers to shop your company, looking for gaps, failures, and any signs of mediocrity you may be inured to.

- Calling 20 or more customers or clients for candid discussions of your business, digging deep to discover what, if anything, they love and what they would want to change.

- Taking a turn as a customer yourself. Call incognito. Visit your website. Place an order. Ask yourself, "Is this truly a thrilling experience?"

The Discovery process peels back the layers of your business to reveal legacy processes and procedures, camouflage, and even subterfuge. You can learn not only what your business does well and where it performs poorly but also why and how certain aspects of your operations evade detection and thus corrective action.

> *The Discovery process peels back the layers of your business to reveal legacy processes and procedures, camouflage, and even subterfuge.*

The Discovery is best conducted as a series of interviews with a wide range of people whose opinion about your business should carry substantial weight:

- Former employees
- Customers

- Former customers
- Prospects you have failed to win over
- Trade associations
- Editors of industry publications
- Securities analysts (if yours is a public company)

As you notice, we do *not* suggest interviewing existing employees, as their opinions are often skewed in ways that distort the findings.

The results of the interviews add up to a view of the business that is of greater value than the sum of its parts. You are presented with a comprehensive look at your company from the outside in, and the results are often unflattering but highly valuable in providing you with a road map for moving forward.

In one of the Discovery sessions MSCO conducted for a group of retirement communities under common ownership, we found that:

- On-site staff failed to project courtesy and a sense of hospitality;
- Prospective buyer tours were conducted with a casual nonchalance that left the prospects with the distinct impression that no one had pride in the communities;
- The residences were considered highly attractive but substantially overpriced; and

- The communities had a reputation for shoddy workmanship, which though untrue, was never corrected in the marketplace.

Throughout the Discovery, identify every single aspect of your operations that simply goes through the motions. Where is there no joy in customer interface? Where do you follow the conventional rules as opposed to reinventing the rules? Do you scale the heights to the level of rewarding your customers with an unforgettable experience, or do you settle for "good enough"?

Step 2: Envision Delighting Your Customers

You could call this the "dream big" step, but it's more than that. This action entails engaging in the process of *Envisioning*, in which you are imagining your business as extraordinary through the eyes of your customers. You're thinking of ways to thrill your customers as opposed to simply serving them.

Einstein liked to say that more important than his scientific prowess was his ability to fantasize about making the "impossible, possible." In the course of his momentous work, he would develop a fantasy (a scientific concept that he knew defied reality) and would then work backwards to reality. You need to "see" where you're going and then figure out how to get there. I call this Cartoon Imagination.

Businesspeople love to say that they want to develop "out-of-the-box" thinking, but with Cartoon Imagination, you start from outside the box to begin with, not inside.

Businesspeople love to say that they want to develop "out-of-the-box" thinking, but with Cartoon Imagination, you start from outside the box to begin with, not inside. If we take a cue from Einstein, we don't have to liberate our in-the-box thinking when we are never imprisoned by it in the first place. Begin with the dream, the fantasy, the seemingly impossible.

Step 3: Learn from Others

Take the cues you identify at other businesses—the ones that leave you exhilarated or feeling somehow deeply impressed—and apply them to your own. Look at how they fight the four factors that cause failure by having:

- Strong, effective leadership
- A culture that is not complacent but continues to lust after customers rather than getting lax
- Competent employees

Also consider how others forego conventional thinking; that is how you thrill your customers.

One thing I learned from a neighborhood business is that customers love it when you treat them as more than special—as divas and VIPs. That may seem obvious, but what may not be obvious is that you do that by breaking the rules. Here's how I discovered this. My wife and I shop at a clothing boutique that is perpetually packed, the parking lot overflowing. Managing a flow of vehicles that must be parked and retrieved minute by minute requires a well-oiled methodology. The attendants need to follow the system—designed for maximum efficiency—to a T.

Or do they? The fact is, the general manager has infused the staff with a drive to thrill patrons and to break the rules to do so—because breaking "the rules" is where the thrill often lies.

As a regular customer, I am never given a claim ticket for my car. In fact, the valets park it right outside the front entrance, making a statement that I am a special guest and ensuring that I can leave within seconds of making my purchases.

This simple gesture, built into the culture, says I am not a customer—I am a houseguest. The company does have a system, management has developed logistics, but I am made to be blind to it. They instead choose to thrill me so that I will come back again and again. And I do.

What rules can you break or bend for your customers?

THE RULES

Early in our lives, we are all handed a book titled "This is the way things are done." The obedient read it and follow it as dutifully as possible. The wise, the innovators, the change-makers read it and then re-write it with their own version of The Rules.

Early in our lives, we are all handed a book titled "This is the way things are done." The dutiful read it and follow it as dutifully as possible. The wise, the innovators, the change-makers read it and then rewrite it with their own version.

Recently, I watched a TV feature about a boy whose twin brother died. The tragedy tossed the surviving twin's life into turmoil and depression. Just as he was spiraling into a point of no return, someone suggested that he visit a pediatrician.

If the doctor went straight to the book and its rules, which likely would have looked to standard medicine as the answer, the boy might not have gotten the help that transformed his situation. But the doctor tossed out the book and instead asked the boy what, if anything, made him smile. Surprisingly, the boy answered in an instant: "Baking."

The doctor encouraged him to begin baking cookies and to start his own after-school business—

and to top it off she took $20 out of her pocket, handed it to him, and announced herself as his first investor.

Today, he is a young entrepreneur with a new passion for life. I believe he will be a stunning success and make us all proud. I believe he has a rule breaker to thank for that. They don't teach that in school. They shun it.

In addition to breaking the rules, another lesson to learn is that building relationships with customers is the key to retaining them.

Considering all the jokes about a doctor's bedside manner, you don't normally think of the doctor's office as where you would learn about relationship-building. After all, we live in an age of medical productivity and doctors are compensated, for the most part, based on the number of patients they see, meaning there is little time for any one person in the examining room.

But it doesn't have to be that way. Not uniformly. One of my doctors, cardiologist Ron Wallach, spends our first ten minutes or so talking about politics, art, business, and investing. It would appear, on the surface at least, that this dilly-dallying would make him less highly compensated than if he got right down to business, examined me, and proceeded to the next patient.

But the opposite is true. His willingness and desire to learn about his patients, to put the stopwatch aside and build a true human relationship, leads to the warm and passionate referrals that have built a booming practice.

In what ways can you make your interactions with your customers more personal? Whether you are a merchant, the CEO of a software firm, an accountant, a fashion designer, or any other kind of businessperson, you can apply the break-the-rules approach to your customers/clients/businesses in a way that moves the relationship from a purely transactional one to a relational one. Take a moment and think about how you can do this. Remember, start *outside* the box.

Step 4: Continually Improve

Seek continuous, iterative improvements in your business. Establish a set of benchmarks to raise your company's performance to the level that delights your customers—and once you accomplish this, raise the bar again. And again.

Sandy Weill was building Citigroup, and my firm, MSCO, was providing marketing services for Smith Barney. At Sandy's office, a sign I once saw there declared, for all of Sandy's team to see:

The Chairman Is Not Happy

This was Weill's unique and unforgettable way of saying effectively, "Don't allow complacency to slip into our company's culture. There are always cracks in our system and ways that we can cut costs, raise the bar on our operations, polish our client services—and I can guarantee you, we're not doing them as well as we can."

Just how right Weill was came into sharp focus when he left the company in April 2006. Although critics believed that Sandy's business model—assembling a sprawling supermarket of financial services—was doomed to collapse, the truth is that under much of the founder's 20-year reign, the company's revenues and profitability soared. This happened in great measure because Weill knew intuitively and viscerally that to grow an ever-more successful enterprise, you must keep the pressure on and maintain the growth spirit with a relentless drive that no one can stop.

7.

Woo Your Customers: The Power of the Thrill

When the pundits were opining on South Carolina governor Mark Sanford's erratic behavior in courting an Argentinean mistress, leaving the country, and going AWOL without notice, a wise observer homed in with amazing precision on the cause of the politico's wild escapade: "He is madly in love with someone new. That always leads to temporary insanity."

It may seem at first blush that Sanford's dalliance has zero to do with business, but in an odd way, it gets directly at the core of a powerful life force that manifests itself (in a perfectly ethical way) in the best businesses—and actually becomes their hallmark.

The first rush of new love is so wildly intoxicating that it blurs one's judgment and prompts the kind of giddy optimism that makes one feel as if all is wonderful in the world, and furthermore that everything is possible; a sitting governor can vanish, lie about his whereabouts, fly off to make passionate love to a mystery woman, and convince himself that no one will know a thing about it.

It can only be ascribed to Temporary Insanity.

Temporary Insanity

In the strange brew that is life, we can *fear* and *pursue* something simultaneously. This seeming disconnect might look a bit bipolar. I mean, who would purposely do that? Do you want to be insane? Of course not. But wait. Do you want the joy of a sensation that is so powerful and exhilarating that it liberates you, temporarily, from the laws of physics—and the confines of daily life—so that the impossible becomes absolutely within the realm of your control?

In the strange brew that is life, we can fear and pursue something simultaneously.

Of course you do. The brand of temporary insanity that springs from new love is so deliciously intoxicating that it drove England's King Edward VIII to abdicate his throne (to marry an American divorcée) and prompts millions who barely know each other to tie the knot at Vegas drive-in chapels.

The Ivy League schools don't teach a single course on love or the sensation of thrill related to it. Nor do   they cover the temporary insanity it can create. This is a shortcoming of immense proportions, not because of the lost benefits to the social sciences or psychology fields, but for the study, insight, and understanding it could bring to businesses. A solid grasp on the power of the thrill illuminates how great businesses attain their vaunted position—and then secure it for generations, as well as provide clues on why they tend not to decline or, if they do lose their bearings, how they regain them.

A solid grasp on the power of the thrill would help show how great businesses attain their vaunted position—and then secure it for generations, as well as provide clues on why they tend not to decline or, if they do lose their bearings, how they regain them.

A Lesson in Love

At a time in my life when I might have gone to Princeton, I went to a far superior university known as Paris. In my brief time living there, I fell in love a dozen times. Each one felt like forever. In every single case, I was magnificently, temporarily insane.

Many years later, as I built my marketing firm and began to fuse the experiences of my life into a business methodology, I reflected on how important it is to provide service in such a way that customers and prospects make the transition from *liking* what my firm had to offer to absolutely *loving* it, and also how key it is, in the course of this transition, for us to thrill them with the quality and depth of the epiphanies I've had over the years.

One such epiphany I've been blessed with is this: if those who patronize your business for the first time or the hundredth do it simply because they *like* your products or services, you will fail. Liking you is not enough. Your goal must be to infuse what you do and who you do it for with so much attention and innovation that the objects of your devotion fall in love. And not simply in love, but go all-out, gung-ho insane, where they believe that they just cannot or will not do without the offerings you are providing to them.

If those who patronize your business for the first time or the hundredth do it simply because they like *your products or services, you will fail. Your goal must be to infuse what you do and who you do it for with so much attention and innovation that the objects of your devotion fall… all-out, gung-ho insane.*

People didn't care that Walt Disney was a high school dropout. They fell head over heels for the films and the Magic Kingdom. And speaking of heels, women don't slide on a pair of Manolo Blahnik stilettos and feel like they made a good purchase. They are sure they just had the best sex of their lives. Why? They are temporarily insane. So much so that they will spend $750 on these stylish shoes and thank Mr. Blahnik for the privilege of letting them do so. They behave this way because this Spanish fashion designer thrills them over and over again.

Great business is when the art and science of romance connect in some wonderfully mysterious way to commerce. What must you do to make it happen in your company? Every day you go to work, you must have one overriding ambition: to get your customers to go "insane."

Not just once, but day after day, month after month, year after year. It starts with temporary insanity and moves along a continuum to everlasting love. That is both the hallmark of a great business—and the thrust of the rest of this book. We all need to get there or we are simply wandering through Medio-creville without a compass.

Women don't slide on a pair of Manolo Blahnik stilettos and feel like they made a good purchase. They are sure they just had the best sex of their lives.

Entering the Thrill Zone

Sometimes in life—and, in turn, in business—the most powerful concepts sit right in front of our eyes and yet we are blind to them.

As business owners and managers, we are aware of and try to achieve such common and noble goals as:

- Customer satisfaction
- High quality
- Courteous service
- A satisfying experience

But the most important goal, and the power it can unleash to distinguish and drive the growth of a business, is almost universally omitted from the managerial handbook. That is the power to thrill.

When a business thrills a customer or client, the relationship this spawns produces enormous energy, organic growth, viral advocacy, and a near-impenetrable barrier to entry.

Working to go beyond satisfactory performance all the way to ensuring that customers are continually thrilled is an intriguing and beguiling compass for achieving a rare state of business supremacy that is:

- A magnet for customers who, once exposed to its exceptionalism, become its viral advocates;
- A daunting barrier to entry more powerful than a proprietary technology or a multi-million-dollar advertising campaign; and
- The virtual license to escape the bounds of comodization in any industry and to qualify for rich and sustainable margins.

A business that *thrills* never does so by accident. It happens when management makes a decision to surpass the traditional business model that is associated with clichés such as:

- Good service
- Reliable products
- Well-trained people
- Customer courtesy

All of the above rules of the standard business playbook are sound and important, but they are simply the price of admission in a competitive marketplace, far removed from the all-important dynamic of exceptionalism.

All Made Up and Looking Gorgeous: How Revlon Won Over Its Customers

From the day Charles Revson launched Revlon with $300, he was driven to the point of obsession to build a clientele, a following, that worshipped the company's products, would gobble up every brand extension he brought to market, and would never tolerate competitors (Revson viewed them as imitators) of any kind. He would accomplish this not primarily with slick advertising campaigns (although he did advertise heavily and effectively) but first and foremost with a religious zeal to create and maintain a product line that exhilarated women in search of what I call the Marilyn Monroe Factor (more on that in the next chapter).

The achievement of a state of thrill can only be born from an unorthodox approach, as anything out of the standard playbook is just that: Standard. Meaning it's ordinary and predictable.

The achievement of a state of thrill can only be born from an unorthodox approach, as anything out of the standard playbook is just that: Standard. Meaning it's ordinary and predictable. Instead of delegating the goal of Revlon's exceptionalism to a quality control group of middle management bureaucrats, Revson took full leadership for achieving the Thrill Factor:

1. He replaced the dyes commonly used in the production of nail polish with pure pigments to provide a vastly superior appearance.

2. He tested the products on his own nails, rejecting the idea that such behavior was unbecoming in a CEO—and a male to boot. Revson knew that the "well-respected" rules trapped companies in the straits of mediocrity.

3. He would man the customer feedback phone lines, determined to hear for himself what women said about his products, engaging them in dialogue, and thus ensuring that none of his managers kept "bad news" from the boss. "The reason I talk to them," Revson said of the customer calls, "is that they are the real boss."

4. He vastly expanded the palette of product colors, recognizing that the ability to make his customers appear original and at the vanguard of fashion would be his most potent asset.

Today, business leaders are distanced from their products and services. Telecom executives run car companies, accountants lead retailers, financiers operate

whatever enterprises they acquire. Most are textbook fig-
ureheads with book knowledge but no sense, instinct, or
passion for the product they are selling and, in turn, its
marketplace. This intellectual and visceral distance from
those you are serving and what you are serving them
renders it virtually impossible to get to thrilled.

Disney's Magic

This gap between company policy and customer aspira-
tion is often the reason once-stellar companies lose their
magic. Walt Disney was driven above all else absolutely
to tantalize his customers. The business he created was
simply a vessel in which he would house his Cartoon
Imagination. Just the thought of people lost in a fantasyland he created—replete with talking ducks and an irresistible mouse—left him giddy and striving relentlessly
to find new ways to thrill and delight. Walt's speech
marking the opening day of Disneyland captured this
exhilaration and the philosophy behind it:

> To all who come to this happy place: welcome.
> Disneyland is your land. Here age relives fond
> memories of the past... and here youth may
> savor the challenge and promise of the fu-
> ture. Disneyland is dedicated to the ideals, the
> dreams, and the hard facts that have created
> America... with the hope that it will be a source
> of joy and inspiration to all the world.

When Disney died in 1966, the extraordinary empire he built fell into the hands of financial engineers, determined to drive profitability at the expense of reinvesting in the thrill factor. Distanced from the goal of enchanting customers, from the dreamlike imagination embedded in the founder's psyche (and, in turn, his business practices), the suits ensconced in the corporate suite allowed a legendary company to slide into mediocrity. Only when Michael Eisner was recruited to take the reins after years of neglect did Disney reconnect to its past and insist once again on thrilling customers, as opposed to simply allowing them to enter the grounds of what had become just another amusement park.

Walt Disney was driven above all else absolutely to tantalize his customers...Just the thought of people lost in a fantasyland he created—replete with talking ducks and an irresistible mouse—left him giddy and striving relentlessly to find new ways to thrill and delight.

Treat Your Customers Like Royalty—or Family

The conventional components of customer service (just the term *customer service* sounds like a chore as opposed to a joy) are light-years away from achieving a fusion of elements that leaves patrons thrilled to the point that they become fiercely loyal and a viral sales force for your business. But some companies, when they go against conventional thinking, have bridged that gap. During a yearlong consulting engagement, I found myself staying at the Fairmont Waterfront Hotel in Vancouver, Canada, for three days per month. I tended to arrive at the same time, eat breakfast, have dinner after my business meetings, and then retire for the evening.

The service was always impeccable, but I must admit I expected it to be that way, given the relatively steep room charges I was paying for the privilege of staying on the Gold Floor.

I *liked* the hotel but was not *wild* about it. The signs of my relative discontent were written on the walls: I tried the Four Seasons now and then, and perhaps most tellingly, never felt compelled to broadcast a sense of pleasure about the Fairmont to friends/family/colleagues. I was happy there, but happy isn't thrilled.

But that would change.

On one particular visit to the Fairmont, accompanied by a colleague from MSCO, I took a late flight out of JFK and arrived at the hotel at 2 a.m.

The night staff had never seen me before, but to my surprise, they all knew my name.

"Good evening, Mr. Stevens."

"Is everything satisfactory, Mr. Stevens?"

"Is there anything special that you require, Mr. Stevens?"

My colleague and I took seats in the lounge to have a cup of tea before retiring. Struck by the fact that I was treated as family by people who were virtual strangers, my colleague felt compelled to decipher the mystery. She took her curiosity to the front desk.

"Pardon me, but how do you all know Mr. Stevens by name?" she asked, pointing in my direction.

She was advised that when a member of the Fairmont President's Club Elite Level is scheduled to arrive, the guest's photo is circulated to the staff so that they can address the VIP by name.

"Where do you get the photo?"

"We simply Google the person or ask the guest's office to send us one."

The Fairmont Waterfront did not want guests to be satisfied. They wanted me and my fellow loyalists to be *thrilled*. That level of detail, of determination to make me feel like a member their family, to prepare on such a personal level for my visit—that was the tipping point.

Vegas-Style Thrills

Steve Wynn understands the power of thrilled and how to deploy it to build stunningly successful businesses.

To many, Wynn is a billionaire entrepreneur who runs a gaming empire. But beneath the surface of that superficial description lies an Impresario of the Thrill—a man who understands how to, and why to, take what is considered to be "the gold standard" and then reinvent it to reach an even higher plane. To close the gap between *happy* and *utterly delighted*.

A graduate of the University of Pennsylvania, Wynn took over his father's chain of bingo parlors when Wynn Sr. fell victim to heart surgery complications in 1963. After taking the helm, resetting the management compass, and demonstrating sustainable growth in the limited world of bingo, Wynn scanned the horizon for a grander stage.

He found it in Las Vegas. A handful of destinations in the world are magnets for men and women of cosmic ambition: Wall Street, Hollywood, Las Vegas, and Silicon Valley.

Wynn chose Las Vegas. Over time, he purchased interests in a portfolio of Vegas gambling operations. He recognized that, for all of its unique characteristics, Sin City was still very much a relatively tame strip of hotels, neon lights, casinos, and restaurants. Wynn was determined to introduce a new dimension, leaving the millions who visited Vegas annually awestruck and thrilled. He would do so with the 1989 opening of the Mirage, featuring an indoor forest and an outdoor volcano. Hotel/casinos didn't have forests and volcanoes in their playbooks, but Wynn wasn't creating a hotel/casino per se, he was unveiling a Thrill Machine. Caught up in the Wynn-orchestrated fantasy, visitors would spend freely and lavishly, exhilarated by the fairy-tale world the maestro created for them.

For all of its unique characteristics, Sin City was still very much a relatively tame strip of hotels, neon lights, casinos, and restaurants. Wynn was determined to introduce a new dimension, leaving the millions who visited Vegas annually awestruck and thrilled.

As the *London Times* has observed:

> *Ever since he was climbing up on the bingo tables as a boy to watch his dad, Wynn has wanted to*

entertain, make money, entertain some more, make
more money and entertain, over and over again.

Moving along this continuum, Wynn proceeded to outdo himself, opening the Treasure Island Hotel and Casino, complete with a live pirate show, and then the Bellagio, with an artificial lake, dancing fountains, and a world-class art gallery. At a cost of $1.6 billion, the Bellagio was the most expensive hotel/playland on the planet.

As a Thrill Maker, Wynn lives more than anything else by the cryptic philosophy his father imparted to him: "Give it schmaltz. They're not coming to make money, they're coming for the show. So jazz it up."

Wolfgang Puck: A Chef Who Thrills

Wolfgang Puck, one of my firm's clients, accomplishes this showman's feat with aplomb. In a nightly ritual that has become his charming and distinctive signature, the Austrian-born chef moves through the kitchen doors while dinner is in full swing and waltzes through the buzzy spaces of Spago, Cut, or any one of the other restaurants in his empire that he happens to be presiding over that day.

Many chefs work the room, but Wolfgang sees it as anything but work. The restaurant is crowded wall to wall with his guests—the people he is determined to thrill on multiple levels—and that is precisely what he does, roaming from table to table (confectioner's sugar on his arms, spots of tomato sauce on his uniform), meeting and greeting, and taking in the lovely theater of delighted people enjoying his delicious creations.

I have marveled at this ever since my first visit to a Puck restaurant more than two decades ago. After all of his success, his fame, his wealth, nothing has changed. On a recent visit to Spago in Beverly Hills, Puck cooked dinner for my wife, Carol, and me, bringing out sumptuous plates of food and watching, like a giddy teenager, as we relished everything. The more we ate, the more we protested that there was no room in our stomachs for more, the more he cooked and cooked and delighted in every bite we took.

Although we flattered ourselves that we were getting the VIP treatment because our firm served his, the truth is everyone in the room was being treated as the only guests in the house. All were thrilled.

8.

Thrill to the *N*th Degree:
Learn from the Masters

A billion women came before Marilyn Monroe. A billion have come after her.

But she has never shared the silver screen or the life stage with anyone. She is a timeless beauty, an exotic wonder woman, a sexual shockwave, and an object of universal lust. And an extraordinary business lesson.

No woman ever stood in a room with Marilyn and felt beautiful. No man ever shared her presence and felt sane. She stole the heart of the most heroic athlete of her time, Joe DiMaggio, himself an American icon. She captured the soul of the greatest American playwright, Arthur Miller. She married them both and then she moved on to Camelot and wrapped the commander-in-chief, JFK, around her finger.

Marilyn is of no distinct period in history. She is known to teenagers and seniors alike, urban and rural, Elton John (who sings beautifully about her) and Vladimir Putin (who adores her films). The world loves Marilyn—even those who pretend they are too smart and sophisticated to admit it.

Marilyn Monroe is irresistible.

A grand painting of the icon commands the center stage wall of my firm's conference room. Whenever new clients arrive at MSCO, I advise them that achieving the level of thrill Marilyn evokes is our goal at the firm. Equally important, she is a metaphor my team members must look at to judge the quality of our work on the like-to-love continuum.

How Great Businessmen Mimic the Marilyn Factor

Recently, I watched a news story reporting on crowds lining up in the wee hours to buy the newly discounted iPhone. Why would they do that? Why did thousands do the same when the product was first introduced? Why have so many millions bought them when they already had cell phones?

Because Steve Jobs has always understood Marilyn Monroe. He has spent his entire career making sure he wasn't selling things people just liked.

Like is a commodity, but *love* is a magnetic force. Great businesses always find a way to transition a product, a company, from like to love to thrilled. If the marketing, the customer service, the product development, the service delivery fails to do that, it is just a glorified way of going through the motions.

Every time you wonder how you can make your business better, resist the temptation to read a treatise from a tenured professor of business management (who has never had a private sector job much less run a company).

Look at a picture of Marilyn Monroe.

Former CEO of Bloomingdale's Marvin Traub was regarded by his 1970s' peers in the business community as a retail legend, but Traub was not motivated to be an exceptional merchant. He had a different ambition. When Traub got dressed in the morning, his thoughts turned to entertainment—specifically, how he would blow you away the moment you walked through the doors of Bloomingdale's flagship store in midtown Manhattan.

Sears and JCPenny's were not Marvin's role models. Marilyn Monroe was.

By deciding how to differentiate Bloomingdale's—by making shopping a thrilling, entertaining experience—Traub turned a once-dowdy merchant into the darling of young fashionistas.

Traub's magic act turned it into a new form of retail theater that viewed celebration, electricity, entertainment—all in all a form of intoxication— as the powerful differentiator.

These trendy customers didn't just shop like addicts at "Bloomies," they virtually lived there, weaving a weekly or even daily pilgrimage to the flagship Manhattan store into their social lives.

Bloomingdale's had been a traditional retailer with stacks of merchandise as the foundation of the business model. But Traub's magic act turned it into a new form of retail theater that viewed celebration, electricity, entertainment—all in all a form of intoxication—as the powerful differentiator. I chronicled this in my 1979 book, *Like No Other Store in the World:*

> *Under Traub, Bloomingdale's success is based on its realization that adults like to have fun too. Ever since management started transforming the store in the late 1940s from a tacky bargain outlet to a top-of-the-line emporium, careful attention has been paid to making Bloomingdale's a place where people could really enjoy shopping. To cater to an adult's version of fun, Bloomingdale's has designed its stores as fantasy-like worlds of exotic gifts, international fashions, and lavish displays. The result is what* Time *magazine has called the "adult Disneyland."*
>
> *In the process of building this quasi-amusement park, Bloomingdale's has revolutionized the ways goods and services are sold throughout the world. The store's contribution to retail science is the movement away from the age-old product-by-product sales system to an "umbrella" scheme utilizing broad themes, promotions, and merchandise categories. According to traditional merchandising methods, which went virtually unchallenged for more than a century, each item in a store had to*

stand on its own. Attempts to tie merchandise together were limited to dividing stores into departments.

In changing this unwritten law, Bloomingdale's managers picked up on innovations that were already taking place in the small shops of London, Paris and New York. Throughout the late 1950s and '60s, the influence of the emerging pop culture produced new and interesting kinds of boutiques in bohemian sections like the Left Bank of Paris, London's Chelsea, and Greenwich Village in New York. For the first time, stores installed jukeboxes, offered unisex apparel, and combined unrelated merchandise lines like health foods and casual clothes under a single roof. As happens in many industries, the small and more flexible retailers were the innovators.

What Bloomingdale's did was to incorporate these new merchandising techniques at the department store level. It was the first major retailer to recognize that department stores could be collections of small stores within a store, that the excitement of the boutiques could be reproduced on a larger scale. Thus, with its great financial resources, Bloomingdale's was able to lead the way in imaginative merchandising.

In a move that was crucial to the store's transformation, management also decided to work with European designers, manufacturers, and vendors to obtain merchandise that would be unique for the U.S. market. Buyers

*for everything from food to fashions to fur-
nishings were dispatched to the continent (pri-
marily France, Spain, Switzerland, Italy, and
Great Britain) to purchase exclusive goods for
Bloomingdale's. A search was also conducted
in the United States for domestically produced
goods with a European flair.*

*To pave the way for the new imports,
Bloomingdale's had to help its customers cultivate a taste and appreciation for European
merchandise. And to do this, it started hyping
an image: the image of a savvy, sophisticated,
and Continental American, the image of a
chic, worldly, and affluent lifestyle. The signifi-
cance here is that an established store suddenly
turned away from the classic solidly American
merchandise its customers were used to (for example, the Ivy League look for men), and said,
"This is what you should want. This is how you
should look—and how you should live."*

Dollars for Your Thoughts

As the CEO of a global marketing firm, I am a true be-
liever in the power of business-building initiatives such
as advertising, public relations, branding, and Internet
marketing—as long as they are guided by a strategic
framework and created at the inception to generate a
powerful return on investment.

However, I know from decades of firsthand experience in guiding companies of all sizes in a broad cross-
section of industries that the urge to splurge on costly

marketing campaigns at the outset must be controlled, because it is far more powerful to invest *brains* than *dollars*.

The good news here comes in the form of a paradox: quite often, the less you spend on marketing (certainly before you develop a code-breaking message that can generate high levels of ROI), the more powerful the force you can set in motion for creating the internal combustion that drives the enterprise. How can this be? By accepting that developing or revising a company's business model so that it thrills its customers and/or clients does not require major infusions of capital. Instead, it takes thought, in the form of fresh, original, iconoclastic, irreverent, unconventional thinking that focuses on and unlocks the mysteries surrounding two key issues:

Developing or revising a company's business model so that it thrills its customers and/or clients does not require major infusions of capital. Instead, it takes thought, in the form of fresh, original, iconoclastic, irreverent, unconventional thinking.

1. What can we do that will truly surprise and exhilarate our customers?
2. How can we change the traditional operating model in our business to one that is truly unique and, in fact, breaks the rules?

This is exactly what Traub, Jobs, and Disney did and why they were so wildly successful.

Time to Reverse Engineer: Mapping It Out

To make the quantum leap from being a business that leaves its customers satisfied (think of that as a C+ in terms of grades) to driving them to the ecstasy of thrilled (A+), you must reverse engineer your company, tracing back from the boss's office, where the view of how well your company does and how that is actually received by its customers is often distorted by its distance from the real world where customers are truly exposed to the experience of dealing with the business.

This is best accomplished by creating a Touch Point Map that analyzes and perfects the corporate experience at every point of interaction with the customer.

What is it like when customers:

- Call your company?
- Visit its website?
- Place an order online or through a call center?
- Shop at your stores?
- Meet with your sales reps?
- Make a purchase?
- Return a purchase?
- Enjoy a meal, experience the service, use the products?
- Lodge a complaint?
- Demonstrate loyalty?

The Touch Point Map scrutinizes each of these issues, rates the experience, assesses the quality, and most importantly, provides the insight to make intelligent moves (based not on whims but on market realities) designed to turn up the jets on the company's performance.

The following is a Touch Point Map my company created for a client in the bath supplies retail/wholesale business.

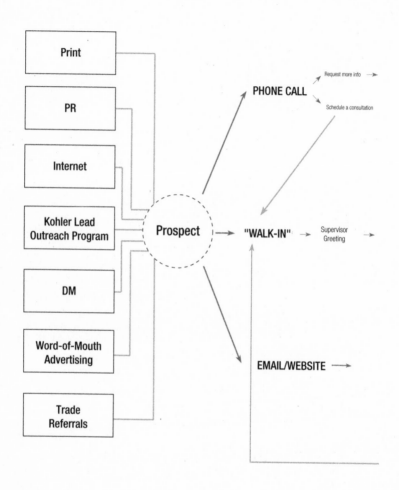

1. Best Brochure
2. Tile Brochure

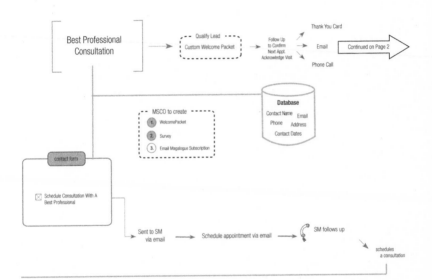

At every point of interaction, the goal must be to get to thrill. To surpass the gold standard. To be relentless in moving the needle to an extraordinary level.

Case in point: every time I visit the Bloomingdale's website to make a purchase with my store card, the system automatically discounts every item I purchase. This says more than *sale*: it declares in words and actions that I am special. Part of a family. Not just another customer. Marvin Traub is long gone from Bloomies, and the business is nowhere near the retailing supernova it was during his tenure, but with this element of surprise, this demonstration of affinity, this *gift* to me every time I buy online, Bloomingdales.com is always on the short list of sites I visit to buy clothing and accessories. And every time I see the retail price shrink as a result of the automatic reductions, I am thrilled. Not for the economics but for the familial quality it implies.

The Touch Point Map assessment provides the no-holds-barred, bare-naked input, the discipline, and the methodology to elevate each component of the customer experience to the power of thrilled.

9.

Does Your Business *Thrill*? Rank Your Business on the Thrill-O-Meter

As you seek to raise the bar on your company's ability to thrill, you need to establish a baseline: where do you stand now, how do you rank, where are you weak, what are your strengths, what actions should you take, and where should you start? The Thrill-O-Meter is a tool for assessing, measuring, and guiding your actions.

Whenever the idea of doing more for customers or clients is raised at a strategy session (and believe me, I have been to a zillion of these meetings), the question comes up: "Do we have the budget for it?"

But the fact is, the challenge is usually not budget driven at all. It's the free things, the intimate gestures, that have the seismic impact on the client/customer experience.

By going to the idea bank before the cash bank, by investing our brains before our dollars, we are forced to think, to strategize, to ask ourselves what we are *not* doing that can create a powerful force in driving our customer to *thrilled*.

L.L. Bean

About 20 years ago, I bought a pair of L.L. Bean boots. I'm an avid, all-weather hiker, and I wanted boots that would keep my feet warm and dry in the rain, snow, sleet, ice—whatever I encountered at Ward Pound Ridge Reservation, one of my favorite wilderness preserves.

Yes, the Bean boot is legendary but I wasn't in the market for a legend. I wanted a sturdy pair of comfortable boots that could take a rugged hike, come hell or high water, and do their job.

I received more than I bargained for, even when measured against my highest expectations. The boots met the icy/wet/wild weather test with flying colors—how they manage to feel like silk slippers in the process is a mystery to me—but that's the feat they accomplish.

The boots are so extraordinary that I have never had to buy another pair. And, if a defect ever emerges, Bean makes good on it, even if they have been hiked in a thousand times.

This may lead you to wonder, "Hmm, if the product is so iron-clad, wonderful, bulletproof, so that Stevens hasn't purchased another pair in decades, isn't quality of that magnitude taking a toll on the bottom line?"

Not at all. In fact, this kind of narrow thinking takes a toll on lesser companies. No, I have not bought another pair of Bean boots, but I have purchased dozens and dozens of Bean's wide range of products for myself, my family, and my friends. Great quality builds loyalty, and that leads to repeat purchases, which becomes an annuity of sorts for the companies that earn it. They transition a sale into an income stream.

Although companies with mediocre or even just plain-old good products can get by for a period of time, the businesses large and small that make extremely high quality a signature of their brand build a following that:

- Keeps coming back year after year;
- Is not vulnerable to competitive attack; and
- Expands its purchases of the company's products, not only in volume, but in depth and width of the product line.

Get to Know Your Customers... and Then Thrill Them

My wife and I use a dry cleaning service in our town that picks up and delivers our clothes twice weekly. The cleaning work is fine: everything comes back fresh, crisp, and nicely presented. But as I have noted, that puts the business smack in the middle of the price of admission-land—fine, but nothing to rave about.

But we do rave about them. And we never look at the prices they charge. And we would never switch to another dry cleaner.

Why?

Whenever the man who visits the house for pickups and deliveries arrives at our property, he doesn't say a word to my wife and me.

This is why we rave about the company?

Yes. Because he proceeds directly to the back of our home, where our golden retriever Blue hangs out, and spends five minutes playing with him. More than that, it seems as if he talks to him.

When a company treats your dog with love, when they tell you in any way that your kids are stars, they thrill the pants off of you.

When a company treats your dog with love, when they tell you in any way that your kids are stars, they thrill the pants off of you.

A realtor I know in New Canaan, Connecticut, follows local newspaper stories of kids who have made the sports teams, were elected class president, have been admitted to Yale—and follows up with the parents, sending them a lovely handwritten letter honoring the child's achievement.

Would you do business with any other realtor? Some will tell you this can only be accomplished by small businesses with a relatively small customer base. Nonsense. It is precisely how many of the once-small companies got to be big.

The trick, as it is practiced by the likes of L.L. Bean, is to always think of yours as a small business, regardless of the sales volume you achieve. In virtually every way, the Bean culture is a small-town shop with a founder stitching up hunting boots in the back room.

At Bean and other companies like it, everyone you deal with at the company is delightful. Every product still comes with a genuine guarantee. A thoughtful "thank you" card comes with orders...even those placed online. Birthdays are remembered. And if you buy a dog bed for your Lab and give her name, they may send her Christmas cards as well.

Once someone sends your pet a Christmas card, they own you. For life. You are thrilled, squared. Because they provide your kids, dogs, cats (and the kid in you) with a memorable experience.

The 360-Degree Customer Experience

Let's explore a word, which represents an issue that businesses spend far too little time addressing. That word is *customer*.

What is a customer? The traditional view of a customer is someone the business serves or sells to. The time has come to rethink this perspective and adopt a model that is simpler in its focus and more powerful in its impact: *The customer is someone we build our business around...to the extent that they are no longer customers.* They are members of the family. Building your business around members of the family, instead of the standard transactional view of serving customers, requires that you make the following transitions in your viewpoint and your actions:

TRADITIONAL WAY	vs.	THRILLED WAY
Meet customer expectations	vs.	Exceed their expectations
Satisfy customers	vs.	Thrill them
Give customers everything	vs.	Surprise them with gestures of thoughtfulness
Give customers access to products/services	vs.	Wrap them in a cocoon of care
Be satisfied if customers like your product/service/company	vs.	Make certain they are thrilled with your product/service/company

As you can see, especially when compared with the traditional business model, the 360-Degree Thrilled Experience is:

- Personal
- Proactive
- Perpetual
- Protective

THE 360-DEGREE CUSTOMER EXPERIENCE

Whenever I meet a new client, I ask them if their customers like their products/services/company. If they say *yes*, as most do, I jolt them by responding: *Well then, you will go out of business.* (That's when they look at me with a question mark on their faces.)

They respond: *Perhaps you didn't understand. I said they do like our company.*

I say: *I heard you quite well. If people like your company, its products, and services, you will go out of business. With so many competing choices available today, they must love it. Because they will regularly patronize only the businesses they love. The ones that thrill them.*

Remember, Liking Is Not Loving. Show Them the Love… with Yogurt?

Making this transition from *like* to *love* is a critical but often misunderstood aspect of managing a stellar business. The temptation and the tendency are to get to *like*, bask in the pride this can bring, and become complacent in its grip. But *like* doesn't *thrill* anyone and only the latter can create the next Richards or Apple.

When Shelly Hwang and Young Lee opened their first frozen yogurt shop in 2005, the last thing the world seemed to need was another place to buy yogurt of any kind. In fact, the entrepreneurs planned initially to unveil a formal English teahouse on their newly acquired, totally off-the-map location at Huntley Drive in West Hollywood, California. But when the teahouse building permit they needed failed to pass muster with the local bureaucrats, Plan B—a yogurt shop—went into effect.

As it turned out, it would be the accidental launch of what would become a business tsunami called Pinkberry—a rising star in the franchise world with outlets multiplying exponentially.

The secret to this exceptional growth trajectory in what many considered a retail niche in decline comes in the form of a chilled thrill: an unforgettable yogurt that is both sweet and tart, created in highly original flavors such as pomegranate and lychee. The store interiors are designed in a casual postmodern/retro fusion that adds to the uniqueness of the Pinkberry experience. From the outset, Hwang understood the importance of creating compelling interior aesthetics, adorning his sleek stores with Philippe Starck furniture and Le Klint hanging lamps.

> *"I would get Pinkberry IV'd into my veins if I could."*
> *—Food blogger Rosie O'Neill*

The company's cultlike following has nicknamed the product "Crackberry" and "frozen heroin juice." Pinkberry is winning over the world because it is more than another frozen yogurt emporium: it is a legal yet addictive *thrill machine*.

Food blogger Rosie O'Neill has captured the essence of the Pinkberry phenomenon best: "I would get Pinkberry IV'd into my veins if I could."

This is precisely the power of *thrilled*—on a spoon.

10.

The Element of Surprise: Only the Unexpected Is Thrilling

It was a gray winter day in mid-February when my son Harly (an automobile freak since the day he was born and whose first word was *car*) asked me if he could see a Mercedes SL up close.

I was a young dad at the time, and Harly and I had this weekly bonding experience other people think of as "going car shopping." The big difference was that we weren't shopping for anything. Ours was a ritual: Harly felt exhilarated being around cars the way wine aficionados feel about strolling through vineyards.

The way it worked was that Harly would devour his beloved car magazines weekly—*Car and Driver*, *Auto Trend*, and *Hot Rod*—and decide by Friday night which car he wanted to "absorb" the following day. This was way serious stuff. We *never* missed a week!

And so it was on this dreary day that Harly was dressed, fed, and ready to go to sit behind the wheel of a luscious new SL 500. It was 9 a.m. and he was ten years old and his determination to get to the dealership was irresistible.

I was a bit concerned how this caper was going to play out. In the usual scenario, Harly and I visited Olds, Pontiac, Chevy, Ford, and other rather commonplace dealerships; we would pretend to be engaged in serious shopping and while I collared the salesperson for a discussion about the vehicle, Harly would commandeer a car on the showroom floor and pretend to be cruising down the interstate.

Today, we were seriously upping the stakes. I knew Mercedes dealers could be a bit snooty and were likely on the lookout for tire kickers curious about how the other half lives. I couldn't see the showroom sheriffs allowing a kid in a scruffy T-shirt and ripped jeans to play Mr. Rich Boy behind the pigskin wheel of what was then a $50,000 luxury chariot.

And furthermore, Harly announced to me that he wanted to go for a ride in *our* SL!

I have always had confidence in my salesmanship, but I knew this would be a major-league test of my skills. And don't forget, this was dad-and-son bonding day. I was his hero. I couldn't fail.

As we walked into Mercedes-Benz of White Plains, the concierge (yes, they have a concierge) asked if she could be of assistance, gestured for Harly and me to have a seat, and promised a sales representative would be right with us.

I could tell that she smelled us out from the start. There was that feigned kindness you can cut with a knife.

Within minutes, the salesman—dressed in a black suit and silver tie—appeared on the scene. Turning my expectation on its head, he greeted us warmly, shook Harly's hand and mine, and thanked us for visiting "my home."

As we quickly discovered, we didn't have the attention of a hired salesman: this was the owner. The president. The CEO.

Spewing forth an absolute lie, I told him that I was interested in buying an SL 500.

> *"It's like no other car in the world, gentlemen ... But don't take it from me. Take one for a ride. Stay out as long as you like. Make sure to do a stretch on the highway and really let her loose. You'll see: the SL is not a car, it's a cat."*

"Do you currently own a Mercedes-Benz?" he asked.

"No. I've thought about it, but ..."

"Have you ever owned a Mercedes-Benz?"

"No, this will be my first."

Then the salesman-in-chief took the element of surprise and squared it.

"It's like no other car in the world, gentlemen," he said, being careful to talk to Harly and me. "But don't take it from me. Take one for a ride. Stay out as long as you like. Make sure to do a stretch on the highway and really let her loose. You'll see: the SL is not a car, it's a cat."

For an hour and a half, Harly and I were in Mercedes heaven. Harly couldn't believe that I let him hold the wheel and I couldn't fathom the fact that I was sitting behind it, guiding a black-on-black rocket ship inside its leather cockpit.

We were thrilled!

I know it was one of the happiest experiences of Harly's life and a combination of mentoring and an inspirational moment for me. That gifted businessman taught me a life's worth of lessons just by handing us the keys to a dream. And by doing it with absolute delight.

He also made me a customer. Although I couldn't yet afford an SL (I've since purchased three from him), I came back two weeks later and bought my first Benz, a 240 D. Once I drove the German wonder, once I was thrilled, once the owner made my son feel like a king, there was no turning back (until my brief flirtation with Porsche).

You know you'd have been thrilled, too. And by now, you should be discovering that you can do the same to your customers. It doesn't have to cost a dime.

We all enter a relationship with a business with a checklist of questions:

- How I will be treated?
- Will I find the merchandise or services attractive?
- Are the return policies fair?
- Is there a genuine guarantee that I will be satisfied or simply a series of empty promises laced with fine print?

Whatever we expect when we enter the company's world, for the first time or the twentieth, management has the opportunity to go beyond the expected, the good, the perfectly satisfactory, and take our breath away. To do something, say something, to make an offer or display a generosity that is 180 degrees from our expectations and truly thrills us.

A card mailed on our birthday? A nice gesture, to be sure, but hardly something that will make you stop in your tracks. Consider how you feel when someone flatters you with a gift at a time you least expect it. When it is *not* Christmas, an anniversary, or your birthday. Just a gesture of appreciation, gratitude, love, or kindness that comes out of nowhere—it has the impact of a first kiss.

Consider how you feel when someone flatters you with a gift at a time you least expect it. When it is not *Christmas, an anniversary, or your birthday. Just a gesture of appreciation, gratitude, love, or kindness that comes out of nowhere—it has the impact of a first kiss.*

Last summer, my wife and I were sitting by our pool when I asked her if she would like me to drive to Starbucks to refresh her with an iced latte. When she said yes, I left the house and returned a half hour later with the drink… and a silver and gold bracelet I purchased at a jewelry store adjacent to Starbucks. I have bestowed her with a zillion gifts on all of the traditional gift-giving dates that intersect with our 35-year marriage—but this "summer surprise" is the one she never forgets.

When Businesses Measure Up

Businesses can (and should) do the same. Richards, a wildly successful apparel store in Greenwich, Connecticut, boasts one of the highest sales per square foot in the retail industry. The place is a phenomenon not because of its goods, its advertising (it barely does any), or its interior design but because of its mastery of The Thrill Factor.

When I was recovering from surgery a few years ago, my Richards' salesperson found out about my illness through the grapevine and moved quickly into action. Understanding the power inherent in the element of surprise, she went straight to a royal blue (one of my favorite colors) Armani (my preferred designer) cashmere sweater, had it gift-wrapped, and delivered it personally to my home (the cashmere sweater on any old Wednesday).

The gift was beautiful, but the real medicine was the surprise visit by a woman who was not going to accept the standard role of salesperson. She was going to thrill me by treating me not as a customer but instead as a member of the Richards' family.

This chain of events was not an accident. The art of the thrill is embedded in a stellar company's culture. (Ah, the power of *culture*.) It is taught, engrained, and exemplified by senior management. Richards' CEO Jack Mitchell—a man who has made his mark and could closet himself in an office or stretch out on a Caribbean beach year-round—still greets customers at the front door, a tape measure draped like a badge of honor around his neck. The silent message: *Nothing in the world would thrill me more than to fit you for a smashing pinstripe Italian wool suit.*

Once Richards gains a customer, it wraps them up in an enthusiastic bear hug and grows the relationship. The element of surprise is one of the super merchant's most potent weapons.

I deployed the element of surprise when I wanted to add Smith Barney as an MSCO client and I did it by, well, insulting them (remember the power of the unconventional).

> *Once Richards gains a customer, it wraps them up in an enthusiastic bear hug and grows the relationship. The element of surprise is one of the super merchant's most potent weapons.*

It was a bold move, telling a prospective client flat out that an aspect of his business was terrible—your company's "marketing sucks" is how I phrased it. The chief marketing officer on the other end of the call could have hung up on me, and he almost did—he was offended and after all, why shouldn't he be? He worked for the prestigious Smith Barney; who was I? I quickly pressed forward and advised that:

1. I was a Smith Barney client.
2. I had substantial assets invested with the firm.
3. I had not reinvested with Smith Barney because the company had failed to continue to educate me on interesting investment options.

After what seemed like an hour of silence but was likely ten seconds, the CMO asked, "Would you come in tomorrow and talk to our marketing department? They need to hear about this. I need to hear about this!"

Within weeks, we were hired by Smith Barney, charged with taking the firm's marketing to a new level. We were filling a void that had somehow been allowed to go unnoticed in the system.

Refuse Mediocrity and Thrill through High-Quality Products

We know that mediocrity derives from a state of mind— one that gets comfortable with the business, its products, and its services, to the point that management entitles the company (by default) to fall behind the competition and the customers.

Call that a prescription for disaster.

Let's take the realm of product quality, for example. Is a *good quality* product sufficient to keep your business growing, thriving, moving, and staying ahead of the curve?

Absolutely not! It has to thrill.

That leads to the question: "What are the attributes of thrilling products?" We have talked about services a great deal to this point. Now let's shine our spotlight on products.

To be a truly *superb* product (over time, all winning products must live up to this standard), a product must provide more than one of the following:

- Stunning innovation
- Exclusive features and performance characteristics
- Irresistible design
- Extraordinary value

11.

The Power of Thrilled: Six Ways to Infuse Your Business with Jet Fuel

W hat we are talking about here is nothing less than an entirely new way of looking at business. It's a way that reverses the traditional hierarchy of actions, issues, and goals and replaces them with a vastly superior order of strategies and tactics that ignite a positive chain reaction with the combustion, the torque, the horsepower, and naked appeal capable of wildly surpassing the norm.

The standard Business 101 textbook order of priorities for building or fortifying a business is to:

1. Create a business plan focused on operational and financial issues.

2. Arrange for adequate financing.

3. Develop or restructure an organization chart and recruit against it.

4. Establish financial goals.

5. Develop an operational process.

6. Create a marketing plan.

All of these are important, even indispensible steps. But the most vital initiative, the Monster Differentiator, is missing. And that oversight is a recipe for failure, third-rate status, or worse. To wit, you must begin the formation or turnaround of your business with a challenging but critical question: *How are we going to thrill customers or clients by offering a truly unique experience?*

If this question is omitted *at the start*, if the answer is knee-jerk or superficial, the company is doomed to mediocrity and suffers a high risk of underperformance—or worse.

Thinking about the thrill at the outset is imperative because of a simple but damaging facet of human behavior: we all say (in what has become a tired and shopworn cliché) that we want to think "outside the box," but we make that pledge with both feet firmly planted inside it, the cover taped tightly over our heads. Once we enter the confines of a constricted (and therefore limited) space, we have to seek to break down the walls in search of fresh air. Once we recognize that the box is always filled with clichés, yesterday's news, stale thinking that's made the voyage from been there/done that and back, we are forewarned to develop ideas that are provocative, dangerous, refreshing, edgy, even impossible—and then work our way back to reality. Starting off with blah means we are usually doomed to stay there—but by launching our thinking, our route to thrilled, with wild-eyed impossibilities strewn across our path—well, that's how we get to thrilled.

This first highly imaginative, no-holes-barred leap-frog toward thrilling customers ensures (and there are few other absolutes in business) that those customers will:

- Be loyal to you as long as you maintain the Thrill Factor.
- Share their advocacy for your business with others.
- Reject the invitations of competitors to switch their allegiance.
- Be willing to pay higher-margin prices.
- Actually share a vested interest in your success. They want you to thrive. You thrill them! The traditional *us* vs. *them* in business becomes a mutual admiration society. Even more—a virtual partnership. A love affair.

Remember Marilyn!

Six Ways to Thrill Your Customers

1. Give them an experience they would never expect from your business. Clients call

on me, at my firm, for advice on marriage, children, personal finances, divorce—even painful psychological issues with which they are grappling. They seek this advice because they know that they are more than clients and I am hardly limited to the role of business advisor. And equally important, they know that the responses they receive from me will be thoughtful, heartfelt, and deeply genuine.

2. When customers ask for service or sales outside of business hours, tell them, "It is always business hours for you." How many times have you approached the door of an establishment, only to have the proprietor flash the "Closed" sign in your face? You can read their expressions like a book: *Too bad. You missed your chance. We're going home for the day.* Wow, that is a sure sign of a company that sucks. And when the proprietor at a similar establishment opens the doors after hours and warmly invites you in—well, that carries the kind of thrill factor you can't touch with a Memorial Day sale.

3. Find out their passions in life and cater to them. When my dad (a nonstop conversationalist) happened to inform a furniture store that he was a fly-fishing addict, the merchant took note and a week later sent a box of handmade flies as a thank-you gift.

After that, Dad would never, ever buy from anyone else.

4. Reinvent your industry's model. This need not be more than a subtle but compelling change. My favorite haircutter sells cufflinks on the display counters instead of hair products—bold and unusual links. I buy a pair almost every time I visit. It turns the haircut into a multifaceted experience.

5. Let the "dangerous minds" in your business loose to act and make waves. Challenge them to come up with thrilling options. At MSCO, we advertise by challenging prospects with the question, "Does your marketing suck?" We even buy print and billboard space with the simple but proactive message: yourmarketingsucks.com. Some don't like what they see, many find it right to the point, no one can ignore it.

6. Appoint a Chief Customer Officer (CCO). This role can be filled by the owner or manager who is dedicated to raising the bar continuously on the joy of doing business with your company.

Let's explore number six in greater detail. For starters, does your company have a Chief Customer Officer? If not, why not?

Imagine giving the customer a voice. Is that too revolutionary for you? At the vast majority of companies, that appears to be the case. Although virtually every major business has a CEO, CIO, COO, CFO, CTO, CMO, the CCO (the voice of the customer) is nowhere to be found.

For companies that live by the rule of the thrill, the Chief Customer Officer/CCO should be at the top of the corporate hierarchy, reporting to the CEO, but with dotted line responsibility to the Board as well. Why? Because just as the CFO must have a fiduciary responsibility to the shareholders, so, too, should the CCO be empowered to identify and protect the customers' interests. And what a difference it makes when the business—ask Southwest Air—puts the customer truly on center stage.

Why do so many companies suck? Because very few companies really think about the customer at the outset or lose their enthusiasm for doing so somewhere along the line. As a result, they never get off the ground in a meaningful way or they endure a slump in the course of their lifecycle. If there was a CCO who really understood the customers' needs:

- Retail establishments would have clean restrooms.
- Interacting with an insurance brokerage firm would be far more satisfying than enduring 18 minutes of telephonic non-human prompts that leads to a dead end.

- Websites would make it easy to navigate, find the information you want, and consummate a transaction.

- When a hotel honors member checks in and asks for an upgrade in a near-empty hotel, they wouldn't be told, "It's against policy."

- You could buy tickets from movie sites without having to remember your password.

- You wouldn't be locked into a two-year contract with cell phone companies and be penalized if you wanted to change carriers.

- Airlines wouldn't have to hold you hostage with points—you'd *want* to fly with them.

A Thrilling Night's Stay

Last year, I was walking through the lobby of the Hotel Bristol in Paris, bags in hand, scouting out a seat in the lounge bar. A thoughtful member of the staff approached me, suggesting that a Bristol guest should not be carrying bags. Although I thanked him and assured him that the luggage was light and all was fine, he insisted on checking the items so that I could focus on a chilled glass of champagne.

He would not take *no* for an answer. And with the seat on the suede sofa beckoning, I happily conceded. My bags were whisked away, I slipped into Parisian happy hour, and it was all as close to perfect as you can get. Think about it:

- This staff member took what others could easily view as someone else's concern and *owned* it.

- A grand hotel, a reigning member of the Parisian elite, takes responsibility for the comfort of each of its guests as if we were family members.

- The rulebook doesn't enumerate the steps the staff should take to exceed guest expectations. They do everything to accomplish that.

- No one is too important to serve as a bellman.

- No one is too busy to perform "menial" tasks. At the Bristol—and the special class of businesses that don't talk service but live it—nothing is considered menial.

The staff member who went out of his way to take my bags deserved recognitfion from the boss, so I brought that suggestion to the front desk. That was when I learned the staff member was the boss—the Bristol's general manager. He is what I call *The Human Ignition Switch*—the leader who, through action more than words, provides a standard for the team to emulate.

What he did is a sure sign of a true leader, one who inspires every employee to raise the bar. To go beyond.

To create the kind of goodwill and loyalty you can't win with gimmicks, offers, sales, or loyalty points. That's reserved for the thrill.

The End of *No*

The single word customers of any business hate most is *no*.

- "No, we can't deliver your order on Wednesday."
- "No, we don't do gift wrapping."
- "No, we don't take American Express."
- "No, we can't make an exception for you."
- "No. No. No."

It's positively deafening.

Think of the "we can't make an exception for you" *no* because it crystallizes the issue. It freeze-frames it, makes us look in the mirror and understand why our companies are falling short of our aspirations for them.

The willingness to make exceptions is precisely what thrills the patrons and prospects of every great business and infuriates those who patronize companies that muddle through (though usually not for long, because they depart for the competition), hold to rules that please themselves, and often take pride in chanting *no, no, no*.

One of the great secrets of companies that thrill is that management eliminates, eradicates, decimates the roadblock, the turnoff word *no* from their business lexicon.

Everyone in the company is taught to find a way, to be creative, to problem solve, in order to turn a potential *no* into a *yes*. And that *yes* often translates into making an exception for the most important people in the world.

Every year, I stay at the Peninsula Hotel in Beverly Hills. In my opinion, it is the best hotel in the United States. Yes, it is beautiful, the food is amazing, and the rooftop pool is a wondrous oasis. But what truly makes the Peninsula extraordinary is that they just don't say *no*. Ever. Under any circumstances.

The hotel has a wonderful policy that if you go out to dine within the confines of Beverly Hills, a hotel car will whisk you off to dinner and fetch you when you are ready to return. Note the fine print of the offer: to enjoy the luxury of the hotel car, you need to dine within Beverly Hills proper. But every time I have asked if management would make an exception and provide the car service outside of the city limits, because the restaurant of my choice that evening was further out in Brentwood or Los Angeles proper, the answer has always been unequivocal: "Absolutely, Mr. Stevens. What time would you like the car, and what time will we be escorting you back?"

Saying "Yes" in the Little Things

Once again, turning *no* into *yes* does not have to play out on a grand stage, with private cars and five-star hotels. Although it is counterintuitive, the *smaller* the gesture is, the *greater* the impact it can have.

Recently, a clothing store opened up in the general vicinity of my home. I live in a semi-rural, historic town, one (albeit an hour away from Manhattan) with meager choices for high-end apparel. So when I ventured over for my first visit, well, let's just say I wasn't expecting to be blown away. No Bergdorf Men's anywhere near quaint old Bedford Village, where you can buy a nice English saddle but where there is nary a suit to be found.

But (surprise, surprise) I could tell from the store window, this shop had genuine promise. I was greeted warmly; the clothing was eclectic and universally interesting. The *piece de resistance* was about to reveal itself. As I was browsing through shelves of cashmere and silk sweaters, I was holding them up for a good look and then seeking to refold them, one at a time, to return them to their proper place.

A saleswoman, who I later discovered was the owner, would have none of that.

"No folding," she declared. "Make a mess. We love messes. Have fun. Try on everything that catches your eye. Leave the rest to us"

"No folding," she declared. "Make a mess. We love messes. Have fun. Try on everything that catches your eye. Leave the rest to us."

And then she sealed the deal (making me a customer and a raving advocate). "If you don't have fun here," she said, "I'm in the wrong business."

We all know way too well what it feels like to have a salesperson tidy up behind us. I think of it as silent scolding: "No. No. No. Please don't abuse our precious merchandise."

This boutique said, "Yes, yes, yes," and ever since I have returned over and over again.

12.

Monetize the Thrill—A Management Road Map

In Pound Ridge, New York—a quiet, historic town a stone's throw from my home—sits a business the vast majority of people would think of as dull, boring, nuts-and-bolts plain. And unable to thrill anyone.

But that's because they have never done business with Albano Appliance and Service. Albano's is the polar opposite of a big-box retailer, selling and servicing appliances such as washers and dryers, ovens, and barbeques.

Virtually anything you can buy at Albano's, you can buy at a thousand other stores. And the store itself is hardly a showstopper—just another neighborhood retailer in a sleepy town that, by any conventional standard, would be underwhelming.

But then you actually do business with Albano's, and the little shop on Main Street dazzles you.

About ten years ago, I bought a Viking barbeque at Albano's. The purchase was pleasant and the staff courteous, but there was nothing remarkable about the transaction. Solid, reliable, seamless.

Five years later, the barbeque needed service and I called Albano's to tend to it. I wanted a technician to come to my home the next day, but I was told I would have to wait two weeks. There was no real emergency, so I agreed and a date was set.

When the tech arrived at 11:45 a.m.—15 minutes ahead of schedule (a first in my experience with a repairman), he was dressed in a fresh, clean uniform, offered to take his shoes off at the door, and went directly to work on the appliance after exchanging greetings with my wife and myself.

As he was working, I asked him why it was not possible to send over a tech before the two-week waiting period.

He said, "We are just so busy that even though we work long hours, we don't have the time to get to everyone quickly."

I asked, "Why doesn't the company simply hire more repairmen?"

He replied, "We'd love to, but we can't find the right people so easily."

I said, "You mean there is a shortage of people capable of doing this kind of work?"

That's when the Albano's serviceman stopped working for a moment, looked me square in the eyes, and asked:

"Would you want someone working in your home who doesn't live in the community?"

Sensing the puzzled look on my face, he went on to explain that yes, there were technicians the company could hire, but the firm believed it had an obligation to go beyond searching for technical knowledge all the way to identifying people who met a high standard for trust and honesty. People who are your neighbors.

Over the years, I have purchased products from Albano's and experienced the company's service culture. It is never jazzy, entertaining, or glamorous in any way. Some companies are not in the business to deliver that.

But in all cases, it is delivered in a way that feels like members of my extended family—uncles, and nephews who are handy around the house—are reaching out to help me. I am confident that:

- They will arrive on or before the scheduled time.

- The work will be performed at the promised price . . . and it will be performed expertly.

- The part of the home they are working in will be left cleaner than it was when they started working.

- I will feel comfortable leaving them alone in the house if I have to go out.

- I will get an honest opinion as to whether or not something can be repaired or is better off being replaced.

No, it's not the same breed of thrilled as staying at
a Steve Wynn hotel or dining at Wolfgang Puck's Spago,
but it is a delight that has made and will keep me a customer for life.

A Not-So-Mountaintop Example

Even great companies can become partially dysfunctional—enough to hold them back from achieving their
maximum potential.

Some years ago, I received a call from the senior
management of Intrawest, a company based in Vancouver, Canada, that had a strong presence in the ski des-
tination business in the United States and Canada. The
company owned and managed such winter havens as
Whistler, Copper Mountain, and Mt. Tremblant.

The reason for the SOS to MSCO appeared to be
straightforward: although the company was performing
quite well, management wanted to drive growth from
$2 billion in annual revenues to $3 billion. The consensus within the enterprise was that the lack of a cohesive
brand linking all of the companies' properties was placing an artificial ceiling on its growth.

As MSCO engaged in a comprehensive Discovery—peeling away the layers of the onion to decipher
the issues under the surface before taking action—it became clear that the problems had little to do with brand
and much to do with management—managerial chaos,
to be precise.

The company was formed around the acquisition of assets, specifically its ski venues and golf resorts. In each case, a general manager was placed in charge of the property once the acquisition was consummated.

The GM had near-complete autonomy to run his business as he saw fit (as long as he produced solid, growing earnings) and his compensation was based on the performance of the asset he managed. In this balkanized arrangement, the GMs bore no collective responsibility for the company's performance as a whole nor could they benefit personally from its aggregate performance.

In this balkanized arrangement, the GMs bore no collective responsibility for the company's performance as a whole nor could they benefit personally from its aggregate performance.

If Whistler earned enormous profits, but Intrawest lost money on the enterprise level, the Whistler GM still had a banner year. For all intents and purposes, he (and similarly for his peers) was a man in business for himself.

This division of the company into unofficially autonomous operating units led to a set of bizarre and damaging practices. For example, visitors to Intrawest destinations were mostly unaware that the company owned more than a single property. If you skied at Intrawest's Stratton Mountain in Vermont, you were under the distinct impression that it was an independently owned venue disconnected from a company with a wide range of ski experiences from which to choose.

This seemingly harmless misconception unleashed a set of damaging repercussions that took an artificial and totally unwarranted toll on Intrawest's revenue potential. When guests tired of annual visits to Mt. Tremblant, for example, or simply sought a change of ski scenery one winter, they wouldn't even think of asking Tremblant's management to recommend another of their destinations—because they didn't have any reason to believe that they had any.

For this reason, when loyal Intrawest customers who adored Mt. Tremblant, Whistler, Copper Mountain, or any of the company's other destinations opted for a change for any reason, their wanderlust would likely bring them to Vail or Park City—popular ski centers but not assets within the Intrawest portfolio. Therein lies the rub and, in turn, the opportunity cost: many skiers seeking new adventures could have easily and happily explored other Intrawest properties as opposed to the competitors, except that no one had bothered to tell them these properties existed.

Why on earth would Intrawest keep its rich lode of assets a secret? As in many cases of corporate dysfunction, it wasn't intentional per se, but leadership simply didn't take the time to identify the built-in limitations of its managerial process and structure.

Specifically, the company did not cross-sell its assets/experiences/destinations because the GMs refused to share their customer databases with each other or with Vancouver-based headquarters personnel. Why would they? Given that their compensation was aligned solely with *their* specific asset's performance, they refused to jeopardize customer relationships by allowing other Intrawest destinations to compete for them. (Even though it was all one company, the management structure allowed personal agendas driven by the company's misguided compensation system to limit rather than leverage the customer base.)

Even if Intrawest had an umbrella brand that distinguished and united all of the destinations owned by the business (which would be infinitely wiser than hiding the common ownership), a proper brand architecture alone would not be enough to promote the collection of assets to customers and prospects actively. The reason is simple but powerful and invisible to the vast majority of conventional marketers: brand alone cannot compensate for a misguided business model.

In effect, Intrawest was a hostage to itself. To please its own general managers, it disappointed its customers, kept them in the dark, and imposed a barrier on its own financial performance. On a fundamental and exceptionally important level, Intrawest sucked. Profitable? Yes, but up against a brick wall.

> *To please its own general managers, it disappointed its customers, kept them in the dark, and imposed a barrier on its own financial performance.*

The Intrawest story is hardly an isolated example of corporate myopia: companies of all sizes, in a broad cross section of industries, fail to inform their customers of the full range of their products and services. As a business grows and evolves, the range and extent of its offerings tend to grow in tandem. Given that this is often incremental and an outgrowth of the lifecycle as opposed to a by-product of a grand strategy, even management loses track of the wider range of its offerings. Because it "just happens" over time, the company often actually fails to comprehend (and define) its own diversity of offerings and, in turn, fails to advise its customer base of the richer selection now available to them. This apparently simple and minor oversight is a major operating/marketing flaw that deprives the business—day in and day out—of its true potential.

In working with clients, it is easy to drive this point home and thus to correct it. For an accounting firm we represent, we gathered together groups of their clients for informal roundtables, our name for casual dinners laced with business conversation. Think of it as living surveys based on frank discussions, sandwiches, and Cokes.

We begin by asking for the clients' view of the firm:

- Does it serve you well?
- Does it leave gaps that it should fill?
- Does its staff ever fail to respond in a timely fashion?

This line of questioning is highly instructive because, all too often, companies have a distorted view (or no view at all) of how their customers see them. By simply asking for an honest appraisal of your business, you actually receive more than that: a road map for mid-course corrections and improvements in your business model.

Our accounting firm roundtables, for example, led to a near-unanimous belief that the firm failed to fully communicate the width and scope of its services

"You don't tell us what you do," was the all-too common refrain from clients new to the CPA firm, as well as those who measured their relationship in decades.

A fast-food master franchisee, for example, a client for years, recognized the need to update its order entry system and to engage an IT firm, referred by a supplier. Only after $375,000 was invested in a system that nearly wrecked the company's operations did management discover that its accounting firm (yes, the roundtable hosts) had a highly proficient IT consulting practice.

"You have been so focused on doing our accounting work for us that you never even mentioned that you engaged in computer consulting," the client said. "Had we known that you have this capability, we would have selected you to do the work hands down. No shopping around. No competitive bidding. You're the ones we know (or thought we knew) and trust."

Does your company fail to telegraph the full extent of its capabilities effectively? It's time to look in your mirror. Do you:

- Hold roundtables of your own?
- Send regular updates on your company offerings?
- Develop cross-selling opportunities by providing customers with incentives for purchasing new products and services from your company?

- Pack orders with sale offers for up-selling and cross-selling programs?

Customers and clients should never have to do homework to discover the full range of your firm's ability to add value to their companies and their lives... Identify what you have and promote the hell out of it.

One of the primary rules of good business, from my perspective, is that customers and clients should never have to do homework to discover the full range of your firm's ability to add value to their companies and their lives. This leads to another axiom that I believe is essential to building and growing business: Don't let your company, or any part of it, be a well-kept secret. Identify what you have and promote the hell out of it.

The Performance Paradox: Teamwork

One of the assets your company may or may not have is an effective team focused on and capable of executing the strategy. Let's put this in perspective. We talk a lot in business about the power of teamwork. Great companies are built, it is said, on the power of exceptional teams.

There is certainly truth to this, but it obfuscates the fact that teams are composed of individuals. And unless an individual is strong, smart, and innovative, his value to a team is minimal. People don't get great because they are joined together in groups; they can only contribute excellence in a way that, in the best of circumstances, makes the group greater than the sum of its parts. Anyone who has ever been naked on a stage so to speak— a ballerina in a solo performance, an executive making a speech, a scientist working in a lab by herself—has to be exceptional *without* a team. With nothing but their raw talent. If they can accomplish this with genius, aplomb, or both, they have passed through a kind of baptism by fire that tests their mettle and, in turn, qualifies them for membership on a team.

Specifically, that means a team that is more substantial than simply a group of people working together. The fact is, mediocre people banded together in an operating unit that muddles through, achieving mediocre performance, is not as much a team as a bureaucracy. In cases such as this, the coming together in a unit of sorts simply provides cover for their individual ineptitude. No one excels, everyone whines, progress and excellence are not in the lexicon. It is called a team, but it is really just a ragtag collection of also-rans blending into each other's woodwork.

Before the extraordinary scientists who made sure America won World War II by creating the world's first atomic bomb came together in Los Alamos, these great physicists had already made their marks, individually, on the naked stage of scientific discovery. For a brief, compelling, and triumphant period, they were willing (for the most part) to cast aside their egos and cross-pollinate their genius for the greater good.

This is the glory and the majesty of an exceptional team. It is a group of talented people, fully capable on their own, who come together to dance *Swan Lake* in a way that thrills the audience or that produces software that breaks the existing barriers on human productivity.

It is one of the great ironies of business that people who pride themselves on being impressed by and supportive of everyone on their teams usually run companies that are anything but impressive in their totality. In sharp contrast, those who are far more critical in their assessments—and the actions they take based on them—are often piloting companies with a sharp edge and a finely tuned quality to all that they do.

Everyone a Shoe-in for Leadership?

Let's explore how this plays out on the front lines of business. It made a vivid impression on me when the owners of a shoe manufacturing company boasted, to my surprise, that they not only got along harmoniously with their company's most antagonistic and temperamental employees, but that they believed they actually added to the company's performance.

Not that the relationship with any employees has to be, or should be, contentious, but I had never heard of virtual sabotageurs portrayed as the secret sauce for creating a superior corporate culture. However, I took the claim at face value and viewed it as a learning experience on my part.

And then, as I worked more closely with the owners and stripped away the veneer of the business, I saw it for the abject failure that it was. Of course management worked joyfully with their adversarial employees: they simply acceded to every demand they made, just as they did to all of their senior managers, who returned the favor with their own staff members.

The company, like many I have seen, was run like a town hall democracy. Everyone had a voice in how business was conducted. That is sound management on one level: giving team members the ability to contribute their thinking to the company leads to a healthy sense of buy-in and collaboration. But companies like the shoe manufacturer that tilt too far in this regard conduct a virtual referendum on every issue. An election, of sorts, where senior management's vote is counted the same as an employee's. What's wrong with that *fairness doctrine*? Just about everything:

1. It undermines the authority of management to the point that there really is no management. Leaders cannot and should not cede to every request nor should they pretend to be just another member of the cast. That leaves the business rudderless.

2. The culture takes on the work ethic of the least creative, productive, and well-intentioned performers. And the hard truth is, the bottom of the staff hierarchy often has little or no work ethic. They report to their jobs, perform their tasks,

and lay claim to a paycheck. On a superficial level, they are fulfilling their obliga-
tions, but companies cannot compete on
superficial levels. Unless the bar is high
and all are required to rise to that level,
and then the standard is raised again and
again, the business goes flat and ultimately collapses.

3. Consider how slacker thinking and act-
    ing seeps through a company. At the same
    shoe manufacturer, the company's sales
    were plummeting over a three-year pe-
    riod. Was a single salesperson replaced?
    No. Was the VP of Sales held accountable?
    No. Was his salary cut? No. Was a freeze
    on expenses put in place? No. Did people
    continue to get raises as usual? Yes, even
    though it wasn't business as usual. In spite
    of the fact that it was an enterprise slowly
    going out of business, management wasn't
    about to change compensation because,
    well, that wouldn't be fair or democratic.

When you see this syndrome developing in your
business—or better yet, when you have the guts to admit
it—you need to take the following action steps:

1. Give up the goal of winning a popular-
    ity contest. Popularity should not be your
    goal; you should inspire your people to
    achieve and then reward them for doing so.

2. Terminate the deadwood. They have been hiding in the ranks for years. Everyone knows it. Send a shot across the bow and a signal to the company that the days of tolerating mediocrity and hostility are ancient history.

3. Gather input from your team if you like, but call off all general elections. It is critically important that you make decisions on your own and stick to them, in spite of the inevitable pushback that will come as you transition from a house of mediocrity to a land of meritocracy.

As you go through this change, keep in mind that the best way to be "nice" to those who deserve this level of treatment is to provide them with an exhilarating environment in which to excel.

Dart Method Doesn't Work

Stellar companies, those with the power to thrill, must peer deep beneath the surface to identify insights into how the company performs and, equally important, how the bar can be raised.

In a typical case, a client of ours was mailing 350,000 postcards every quarter to generate leads for their sales force of insurance agents. No one described it as such, but the hope was that if they tossed enough darts against the wall, enough would stick to provide the agents with sufficient leads.

And then we came upon the scene. Knowing full well that this crop dusting approach is lazy and generally ineffective, we developed a more powerful strategy that would cost more from a per-customer acquisition perspective but would lead to more customers in the sold column. And given that each insurance customer had a long and significant lifetime value, investing in the higher customer acquisition cost made all the sense in the world. The truth is, when you engage in marketing of any kind, you cannot *save* your way to success. You need to find code breakers that deliver high ROI and invest heavily in them.

Now, on to the insurance company mailers. Before we put our new strategy in place, we put ourselves in the prospective customer's place to see what the prospect interaction experience was like. And it was beyond poor, beyond sucks; it was at a level of near-negligence.

The company positions itself as the platinum standard in quality, highly personal insurance firms, and in practice, it is. But when MSCO called the telephone numbers on the mailers, we found call center people who were poorly trained, confused, using broken English, and instead of providing the royal greeting one would expect from a company holding itself up as the premier provider, we were subjected to a rush to quote a price. And even worse than that, when questioned about their offerings, the call center (which worked for other insurance companies as well) offered competing carriers' products as well as those of our client! So, our client was paying to generate leads for competitors.

Does that ever suck!

This is reflective of the fact that so many business wounds are self-inflicted. We can rail against the sun, moon, stars, fate, and Walmart, but through ignorance, arrogance, or oversight, we take a toll on the businesses we love.

I don't know how to explain some of this self-defeating behavior, but I do know how to address it. You can't make this stuff up. One of my clients launches staff meetings by torpedoing the team members in attendance. I mean actually humiliating them in a vainglorious attempt to quash *their* egos and pump helium into *her* own.

So many business wounds are self-inflicted. We can rail against the sun, moon, stars, fate, and Walmart, but through ignorance, arrogance, or oversight, we take a toll on the businesses we love.

The black opera always begins with a rant fused with a trumpet flourish, declaring that she is the mainstay of the company, the driver of growth, the pillar that holds up the entire structure. The goddess speaks and all are expected to absorb and pay homage:

"I'm a supernova and all the rest of you are dim lights in a vast and anonymous universe."

The egoist at hand is actually a highly intelligent woman, loaded with advanced degrees and an acutely sharp mind. But that same cerebellum goes AWOL when she addresses her people—when she *fails* to lead them.

For all her brainpower, she doesn't understand the Pygmalion way—that if you denigrate your people out of sport, you will create a culture that lives up to (or shall I say, lives down to) the insults you hurl at it. After the *great woman* spews her intellectual venom, her team members silently search for ways to sabotage her business. This *always* happens when a terrorist in a suit rules the roost. Revenge becomes the invisible strategy.

Now consider what happens when you take a diametrically opposite approach. When you break the mold and stretch the envelope to embolden your team, extraordinary dynamics are unleashed. Free radicals! RE/MAX became the largest real estate brokerage firm in the world by creating a business model that established and touted its agent force as the elite of the industry:

- No part-timers
- No beginners
- No mediocre performers

Unlike the typical structure at real estate brokerage firms, where agents pay a share of their commissions to the brokers, RE/MAX's founding concept held that their brokers would retain the industry's most generous share of the commission.

The nuclear, game-changer message behind this novel business model was that only those premier brokers who would sell and sell regularly, vastly exceeding the norm, would be entrusted with the RE/MAX brand and, related to this, would claim their commission treasures.

In essence, RE/MAX would be positioned as the home of the best and this sense of superiority—think of it as planned elitism as a business strategy—would drive the agents to excel, if for nothing else than to live up to their brand, confirming their self-imposed stature as the royalty of real estate.

When management of any company builds the morale of its people, when it presents them as the premier providers, it secures the following advantages:

- People find ways to outshine and outperform the competition.
- They exceed the conventional *ceiling* on performance.
- The company's culture morphs into the Standard of Excellence.

A business model of this magnitude requires confidence and optimism—two ingredients that are often missing from companies. And the lack of those are part of a major reason a company never truly takes off or why it hits a wall.

The Wall Is Really Just a Failure to Look Up

Oh, *the wall*. I hear about it hundreds of times a year.

Businesspeople wail that their companies have "hit a wall," growth has slowed or come to a halt, and they are beside themselves. They blame this apparent dead end on all manner of culprits:

- The economy sucks.
- It's been a bitter winter.

- It's been a sweltering summer.
- People are not in a spending mood.
- Credit is tight.
- Competition is relentless.

Of course, there may be truth to some of these boogey-men, but they are never reasons to accept the idea that your business has to endure a period of slow or no growth.

The truth is, *the wall* is a myth. A mirage. And even worse, an *excuse*. Just when you believe your business has hit the wall is the exact time to drive through that mirage with a Ford truck. With your raw will, decide to succeed in any environment, under any set of circumstances. And the best way to accomplish this feat is to thrill people to the core.

The Danger of the Domino Effect

You may take solace in the fact that your company does not suffer from a full litany of damaging patterns and dysfunctional behaviors. But bear this caveat in mind: typically, the slide into abysmal performance begins with a single flaw or weakness that causes a key pillar to crumble, leading ultimately to a full-blown domino effect.

We all witnessed this syndrome writ large in the U.S. auto industry. Although much has been written and discussed about the decline of the once-mighty Detroit, the story of how it all began and spread like a plague throughout the Big Three is instructive as a business lesson—or perhaps as a red flag to everyone who owns and manages businesses.

In Detroit, the slippery slope started with complacency about product quality. Without real competition from other nations, particularly Japan, American carmakers took their domination of the market for granted. Slowly, but undeniably, quality deteriorated, leading to poorly produced products that lacked even the basics, such as meticulous fit and finish. That's a sure sign that the customer (the "lowly customer" from Detroit's perspective) didn't count very much to the hidebound suits holding court on the executive floors of the GM building.

But the industry didn't suffer to the point of disaster due to product quality alone. That's because corporate dysfunction at companies of all sizes never stops at the point of ignition; in typical fashion, as GM's defects and recalls mounted, customer complaints and then outright hostility boiled over. Slowly at first, but then with increasing pace and fury, the media joined the fray. Story after story battered once-proud brands such as Cadillac and Chevrolet, further fanning the flames of discontent. Dealers were pulled into the deepening fiasco, viewed as sleazy purveyors of third-rate, often-dangerous products.

In this cauldron of anger and contempt, hostility spread and tempers flared. In the factories and the executive offices, employees felt besieged. Morale plummeted, taking quality and service to new lows. The only thing thrilling about these moribund companies was the chance to drive past their showrooms and slip into a new Toyota.

The key point is that it wasn't quality problems alone that caused the Big Three to be voted into the Hall of Shame. Once a critical part of a company is allowed to deteriorate, it takes everything with it.

There isn't a company on earth that is perfect or even close to it. Perfection is an unattainable goal that should be replaced with the determination to achieve and maintain a state of excellence that continuously thrills and vastly exceeds expectations. The only way to attain and sustain this position is to a) demand and secure excellence, and b) relentlessly and undemocratically address cracks in the system at the first hint of trouble, preventing what appears to be an isolated issue (but rarely is) from setting off a chain reaction.

We can all slip into states of myopia and/or denial, but recognize them or not, the warning signs always come. The question is, does management heed or ignore them? If GM had simply listened to its customers and demanded that its managers produce quality products, customers would have remained happy, the media would have remained adoring, and the morale of the men and women who produced the most popular dream machines in the world would have remained sky high.

I see this happening to a small hotel, once a gem, right now. In the summer of 2010, I visited the Mayflower Inn, a lovely place my wife, Carol, and I have enjoyed for 15 years. It is country elegant, sophisticated, and understated with excellent food and superb service, the ideal getaway.

But on our most recent visit, something was different. The rooms were wonderful as always. Ditto for the grounds, the pool, and the food. But something was missing. At first, we couldn't put our finger on it, but then it jumped out at us like a neon light: instead of thinking ahead for everything we could possibly want

(SOP at the Mayflower over the years), we had to keep asking and waiting for the staff to catch up with us. Ice water at the pool? Wait. Lunch menus? Wait. A glass of wine on the room patio? Wait.

The fact is, we didn't feel like family, which was always the invisible factor that added so much to the Mayflower experience. Our visit was nice but not great. And we had long ago come to expect great. To be thrilled.

The day after our return, I received an e-mail survey asking me to assess our stay. I answered in one word: disappointing. I didn't know if anyone would pay attention and by this time, I didn't much care. And then the next day, I received a response from the general manager, asking if we could speak. It was a holiday weekend; I was at home and provided my number.

Here's how the conversation unfolded:

> GM: I was disturbed to see your message. Would you be kind enough to explain what you found lacking?
>
> MS: It's a very subtle thing, but we didn't feel like family. Your staff, some of them new, just didn't seem to care.
>
> GM: I feel terrible to hear that. Can you provide specifics so that I can address them all with the staff, please.
>
> MS: I will, of course. But you have a broader issue, and a more dangerous one, than a series of tactical flaws. When I say that your people don't seem to care, that's a cultural issue that,

between you and me, takes some soul searching, investigation, and…well, I wonder If the
person who reports to you on daily operations
isn't asleep at the wheel. And why you don't
seem to know that what was once a gem of
a place, yours, is in danger of becoming just
another inn.

The GM did not view this as a gripe. He identified it
as valuable input and as a wake-up call. He assembled a
team meeting, dug into the issues, made a series of staff
and procedural changes, and put himself on a higher
state of alert.

And he invited my wife and me back for the royal
treatment, compliments of the house.

This was a man who understood that "isolated" problems can quickly metastasize unless they are stopped
cold and reversed. And that the art of recovery with a
customer is a powerful force in the drive to the state of
thrilled.

Creating and maintaining excellent companies, avoiding the pitfalls that lead to their decline, takes more than
flamboyance and highly imaginative minds. More than
anything else, it means doing all of the little things right.

Once exceptions are made and flaws are overlooked,
the slope gets very slippery.

Constructing Positive Customer Relations

A Texas-based home construction business knows full well how slippery that slope can get when, as in many family-owned companies, civil war has set in. Founded by Rob, the youngest of four siblings (all of whom grew up in a loving home nurtured by attentive and adoring parents), the kid brother proved himself to be a natural businessman. After launching the company on a shoe-string (financed with less than $100,000), his "Keep it Simple, Keep it Affordable" concept for building the American dream scored with working-class consumers, driving double-digit growth year after year. Soon after the juggernaut hit revenues of $30 million, Rob gener-ously (but stupidly) brought his brothers into the fold, one at a time, as each sought to participate in the profit machine he had created.

And just as the real-world script so often evolves, once the company became a family affair, all of the ties that bound the brothers since birth unwound in an in-creasingly ferocious and ugly bout of sibling rivalry. Given that Rob made the fatal blunder of anointing his brothers not simply as employees but as partners (always the granddaddy of mistakes), the war that erupted took place in an environment where everyone was now en-titled, not merely by mindset, but by corporate bylaws.

And true to form again (ugly and damaging form), where the company was once a guided laser directed at the marketplace, now in the partnership era, 90 percent of the meetings, e-mails, discussions, memos, and actions had everything to do with protecting each brother's power base and nothing to do with improving the product, developing innovative designs (once the company's signature), or engaging in powerhouse marketing.

The War Within now trumped The War Beyond the company's embattled walls. When this is the case, the only thrill is to score points against internal adversaries. The customer is hardly on anyone's radar screen.

The problem, the damn disaster, is that the War Within is never the one that counts. The products this war produces are office politics, turf protection, and power grabs.

Not a pretty picture, of course, but it never fails to amaze me that all of this is considered part of doing business. Once the culture turns adversarial, the internal battles are thought to be an inevitable fact of life in the world of commerce.

Nonsense. It is an abomination that should never be tolerated. It is the ruination of once-vital companies that begins and ends by diverting the focus from the battle for success and for supremacy in the marketplace to a petty parlor game where winning brownie points becomes the overwhelming obsession.

It is amazing to me how many managers not only tolerate The War Within but provoke and/or engage in it. Here's the list of destructive actions (or lack of them) that turn companies into infernos of misdirected energy, talent, time, and dollars and that must be stopped in their tracks stat:

1. Conducting e-mail wars inside the company. This embeds itself in the culture like

a lethal virus. Blackberrys become weapons of war.

2. Allowing people to undermine their managers by circumventing them and launching appeals to the manager's boss. This *approval shopping* leads to the total destruction of authority and discipline. Owners and CEOs often tolerate or eagerly empower it because they secretly enjoy the power trip that comes with being the ultimate authority people turn to. But in time, the fuse burns out, and the shallow ego gratification gives way to chaos and destruction.

3. Empowering whiners to rant about their co-workers. (I have always made it a rule that if an employee wants to talk about a peer, they must bring that person into my office with them. Net result: no one rants.)

4. Managerial indecisiveness. This leads employees to engage in a guessing game as to where the company is headed and who is heading it. In this sea of confusion, people tend to fight among themselves for the power those above them relinquish by default.

5. Managers who change their minds every time the wind shifts in a new direction. To employees, it appears (and this is often the case) the managers are ceding to the demands or requests of their peers. When

this happens, the company collapses into
a free-for-all.

If you see yourself or your company in this picture,
view it as a warning sign. A reality check. A painful but
reliable indication that the battle to achieve dominance
and turf protection within the company is distracting everyone from the real mission: to give all you have, individually and collectively, to being smarter and faster than
the competition.

13.

Is Your Company More Than the Sum of Its Parts?

In becoming an entrepreneur, I've made every mistake one can make through trial and error. As I work at building a successful business, I still have to be relentless in the quest to maintain my company's excellence and to repel the natural forces that can reduce even the finest companies in the world to mediocrity—or worse. That means that your company, mine—*any* company at any and every point in its evolution—can suck.

The solution is to admit it ("Okay, my company sucks at this point in time") and then to act creatively and decisively, taking constructive steps to address the deficiencies and leverage the strengths. This is never easy, first and foremost because we must come to terms with our failures, shortcomings, disappointments, and egos. And once we scale that wall, we need a compass to guide the turnaround.

I remember one point in the early days of building MSCO. I had hired my first senior employee, a bright and creative woman with a prodigious work ethic. I loved to collaborate with her, to see the sparks fly, to make one plus one equal three when we put our brains together and pulled amazing strategies out of thin air. We were on this intellectual roll, fueled by a give-and-take col- laboration, and the joy ride (mixed with the commercial rewards it produced) was a thrill.

She spent her days serving major clients, acting as their big-picture advisor, and at the outset, they all adored her as much as I did. Original thinkers, we all knew full well, don't come along every day. When they do, and one has the opportunity of working with this rare breed, it is an enthralling experience.

But then the cracks in the picture began to appear, turning Ms. Perfect into just another well-educated woman with more than her share of frailties. In what I can only attribute to a strange and severely disappointing defect, she would consistently fail to finish projects. If a strategic presentation was set to be 50 pages, she would always, always, get to 49 pages and stop, make excuses, lie, promise page 50 was coming, try to cover her trail through alibis and subterfuge—but she would never de- liver that last page.

For months on end, clients would call me asking, "What kind of sloppy business do you run?"

I kept asking my associate to change her ways. I kept making excuses for her. I kept hoping things would somehow get better. But they didn't—because I refused to see that the employee I held out as a gem was really a smart, creative, and hardworking *liability*. And I failed to take the only step that would truly put an end to the problem: replace her.

My company sucked and it was my fault.

Ultimately, I did go on to replace her and to set the wheels in motion (with new hires and revamped policies) to turn a company that sucked into one that hummed. And ultimately, into a growing enterprise that was better than the sum of its parts—that had an exponent over its name.

So I talk not from a pedestal but instead from the crucible of the special kind of hell you go through when the business you manage is third-rate. When it sucks.

This kind of baptism by fire has enabled me to graduate from a set of learning experiences and epiphanies into the development and implementation of an overarching philosophy and boots-on-the-ground methodology for driving superior corporate performance.

Viewed through the prism of my experience, companies fall into one of three categories:

1. Less than the sum of its parts.
2. Equal to the sum of its parts.
3. Greater than the sum of its parts.

The fact that Number 1 sucks is likely apparent to all. Nothing that adds up to less than the sum of its parts can be of any real value. The idea that Number 2 (equal to the sum of its parts) also fails to meet the test of acceptability may be a surprise. But I have no doubt that this is true.

Think of it this way: for years, I have loyally and lovingly patronized a certain restaurant in San Juan, Puerto Rico, where I vacation annually. For years, one of this restaurant's true charms was that it was nestled in a cool and edgy location in San Juan. The exceptional environment's paintings flowed into the eatery and, fused with the chef's innovative cooking, created a total dining experience that vastly *exceeded the sum of its parts*.

On a recent visit to the island, I was surprised to learn from the concierge at the Ritz-Carlton that my favorite restaurant had relocated to the lobby of a San Juan hotel. Crazy about the food and the staff, I made reservations for three nights of my six-evening stay at the relocated restaurant, confident that the flame would still be lit.

Wrong! Situated next to a noisy casino in a second-rate hotel, my favorite restaurant made the reverse transition to a still-good restaurant but without the exponent that had put it near the top of my favorite eateries around the world. I missed the once exotic setting. I wondered why the intense art that gripped you in the former space now looked like wallpaper. Even the staff, gracious as always, seemed to be deflated by the change of venue.

The new version of the restaurant was, to me, equal to the sum of its parts. Did it suck? Technically, no. It was fun, the food was good, but the love affair that had me addicted to the place was gone.

The salient point is that I canceled the two additional nights I had reserved there, tried a place I had avoided during my only-eyes-for-that-other-restaurant love affair—and the experience ignited a new loyalty. Now it was Il Mulino that had an exponent over it!

I gathered that my old favorite had moved to take advantage of a lower rent option. Costs are, of course, important in business. But we must always ask ourselves what expense reductions will actually cost when measured against the toll they can take on customer appeal. In the case of this restaurant's change of venue, it lost my patronage.

The owner should have detected this and he should have declared war on his decision to relocate so that I (and others) wouldn't have encountered the disappointing experience.

Phantom Employees

Paradoxically, in many cases, the Declaration of War that must be announced from time to time must be focused on an individual, a culprit, a force who is not officially an employee of the company.

Take the case of the archetypical family-owned businesses. The founder claims to be in retirement—and in fact, may no longer be on the W2 payroll—but in actuality, has simply relinquished his title and his corner office while continuing to exercise the most insidious type of power: manipulating, second-guessing, and vetoing (without the dignity and process of an official vote) the decisions of his successor (usually a son or daughter).

This charade creates a surrealistic environment where the offspring "in charge" is really a puppet for the parent who can't bear actually ceding control. This leads to a black comedy, culminating in a once-robust business inevitably coming apart at the seams:

- There is a wholesale lack of order, direction, and process. Employees are confused about whose orders to follow.

- Even worse, employees play both sides against each other, agreeing with whoever they are talking to at the time. In the vast majority of cases, there is no venal intent here. The family feud turned power struggle forces the team members into this survival mode.

- To further compound a bleak situation, the entire team loses respect for the two managers (the one now occupying the spacious office and the other pretending to be in exile).

As this destructive pattern plays out, a Shadow Government forms, one that has no meaningful title or defined managerial responsibility but that wields power through equity ownership, parental influence, or, in the most egregious scenario, both.

The existence of a Shadow Government (the founding parent and his/her palace guards) is highly destructive due to a set of odious factors that compound one another:

- The CEO (the son or daughter of the founder) and his team are essentially puppets. They make decisions, announce

them to their team, and then are coun-
termanded by the legacy of the past, still
rearing its head in the present.

- This leaves the team, ostensibly in place
to execute the strategy of its leadership,
with two sets of often-conflicting instruc-
tions, one from the CEO and another from
the Shadow Government. Over time, confusion reigns and turns into chaos. The
question looms over the company like a
cloud: who do we follow? The boss or
the Shadow Government, which like the
Wizard of Oz, operates from behind the
curtain.

- The CEO becomes frustrated, angry, and
often loses confidence in her decisions
and, even more damaging, in her ability to
control and run the company.

- As the situation spirals into ever more per-
ilous levels of dysfunction, employee morale deteriorates as the company becomes
essentially leaderless and rudderless.

- In this vacuum, employees develop agendas of their own. In effect, it is not one
company but several units operating without a central philosophy, culture, or command structure.

Due to this, the customer experience varies widely,
depending on who the specific customer works with
within the organization. This, too, may be perplexing,

as a customer enjoys a rewarding experience in one area, such as sales, and is then treated as a stepchild in the service department.

Quite often, cliques and cabals develop, with some loyal to the CEO and others (often those who have been with the company for years) linked to the Shadow Government. This leads to a constant state of internal debate and conflict, deflecting the company's focus from the marketplace to its own internal bickering.

In time, this always proves to be a doomsday scenario—but one that can be averted if decisive action is taken to reverse course and reclaim control of the business. Every company operating with two power bases is a broken organization, which makes it absolutely necessary to declare war. The CEO must take the following actions:

1. Confront the Shadow Government with an ultimatum: either you cease and desist in undermining me or I will force the issue (legally, if you have the equity or bylaws power to do so) or I will quit (this show of resolve is often enough to get the Shadow Government to back down, as it really does not want to run the business full-time.)

2. Gather employees and make it clear that you are the boss and that you will not tolerate anyone taking orders from others nor will you brook team members developing agendas of their own.

3. If your orders are dismissed as just so much talk, terminate anyone who is a leader of the opposition. This demonstration of strength and resolve sends a clear signal that insubordination and the chaos it unleashes will not be tolerated; order is being restored and you are in charge.

You not only win the battle—you win the war.

14.

If You Were Handed the Company, Chances Are You Don't Know How to Run It

Some years ago, I was called by the president and owner of a hair products company who asked me for an emergency meeting.

I didn't know the guy, never heard his name, never bought his products, never met him or talked to him before, but he wanted an "emergency meeting."

That apparent melodrama always sets off an alarm in my head (I'll get to the reason for that in a moment), but I was willing to meet (a great part of the joy of business, of life, is seeing and cultivating the unknown). I visited the company's website. It appeared to be a legitimate business. Intuitive navigation, clear value proposition, and solid client references. So far, so good. Guiding companies and their management through difficult straits is certainly a key part of what I do, so sure—I would meet with the president.

We got together in Chicago about a week after his call and from the moment we sat down together, he proceeded to tell a tale of Shakespearean woe.

The Laundry List of Woes

The litany of things gone awry was long and painful:

- The sales manager failed for years to meet his goals; therefore, was he fired? Not even close: he was asked to work less, was allowed to relocate out of the marketplace, to have little or no contact with the sales team he was supposed to manage, and kept on full salary. (You can't make this stuff up.)

- Retailers who carried the company's products were pleading and then demanding that the company offer lower-priced versions of its legacy brands (which, due to offshore and Internet competition, had been experiencing declining sales for years). But revised pricing and low-cost brand extensions—meant *change* and the owner detested change, so he rebuffed the retailers, who accelerated their flight to competitors.

- The plant manager, a veteran employee who truly loved the company, offered to take a pay cut in return for the company stepping up its marketing activities in a highly competitive market. In effect, an employee stood up in the ranks and volunteered to subsidize the company's growth. He loved the business, the only employer he had ever known, and wanted to see it regain its momentum. But the president, who had a prejudice against marketing (without really understanding what it is), rejected the idea, deflating the hopes and aspirations of his team and placing the company in an ever-deeper hole. His subliminal message: "I know best. You don't. Shut up."

But the president, who had a prejudice against marketing (without really understanding what it is), rejected the idea, deflating the hopes and aspirations of his team and placing the company in an ever-deeper hole. His subliminal message: "I know best. You don't. Shut up."

The list of managerial/leadership sins goes on and on, but let's get to the cause of this all-too-common multifaceted fiasco: the owner was not an entrepreneur—not a businessman in any sense. Like so many who *run* companies but do not manage them or inspire their people, he had inherited the company from his uncle, who took him under his wing after his father's death at the age of 35.

That's a wonderful gesture and lovely act of kindness (or so it would seem at first blush), but it is often a major blunder that places a person (the beneficiary of a family business) in a position in which he or she is doomed to fail.

So often, companies are lost in the woods because the people at the helm are there through charity as opposed to personal drive and/or meritocracy. They are thrust into a role they are absolutely unqualified for and the business they inherit suffers for it.

If this sounds uncomfortably familiar, it may be because you don't (this is hard to admit) know how to run a company and you are desperately in need of a collaborator/mentor/partner who can guide you.

A key starting point in the development of a strong effective managerial collaboration is the very definition of the company.

Put It in a Phrase

The thrill doesn't have to be glamorous or glitzy. As Sam Walton proved from the start, people can be as thrilled about bargains as they are about diamonds.

Great companies define themselves in sentences. They have a singular but powerful way of differentiating themselves (such as Walmart's "Low Price Leader" or De Beers's "A Diamond is Forever"), and this crystallized message separates them from the pack and places them on the all-important short list. The thrill doesn't have to be glamorous or glitzy. As Sam Walton proved from the start, people can be as thrilled about bargains as they are about diamonds.

When I say that great companies define themselves in terms of sentences, the converse is also true. Companies that really don't have a singular selling proposition write pages (sometimes tomes) about themselves and it's like throwing everything in the fridge into a blender and winding up with gobbledygook. Visit 20 websites randomly, read the *About Us* section, and see if you can figure out what they mean. If by some miracle you can, write them a brief note. They'll be delighted that someone figured it out.

So the question is, how do you create that *one* sentence that captures the essence of your company, a message that serves as a ticket to the short list, and in turn a knife-sharp competitive weapon?

Often, it is the opposite of what logic and/or intuition would suggest.

Managing Is Always Challenging

Managing a business means engaging in a continuous process of learning, of discovery, of achieving successes, and colliding with failure—and using this grand opera of experiences to achieve continuous improvement. To test your mettle, see where it is weak or vulnerable, and find the strategy to make it just right en route to making it right again. Strive for constant self-improvement for you and your team. And as simple and straightforward as that would appear to be for anyone who runs a business, over and over again, I see an ugly and almost unbelievable pattern evolve, as the person in charge flips the autopilot switch and believes that is the equivalent of managing. They just let the business coast, dealing with every challenge, change, threat, adversity, and opportunity as something that will somehow just take care of itself.

The degree to which this distorts the operations of the company and destroys its potential is paradoxically both staggeringly tragic and absurdly comic.

Consider the plight of a beauty supply company run by the daughter-in-law of the founder. The old man had so many successful companies housed within his personal portfolio of entrepreneurial triumphs that he started handing them out like hors d'oeuvres to his family members.

Virtually overnight, the companies stopped performing like capitalist entities. Instead, they ebbed and flowed with the prevailing winds. No strategy. No accountability. No rules. No drive. All because there was no management in anything but title.

At the outset, the transfers were a charade, as the founder kept the businesses he appeared to dole out on a short leash, making all of the key decisions himself. As long as there was entrepreneurial DNA on the scene (his, to be exact), the ruse would not take a toll on the companies.

But then he died. It was a game changer: virtually overnight, the companies stopped performing like capitalist entities. Instead, they ebbed and flowed with the prevailing winds. No strategy. No accountability. No rules. No drive. All because there was no management in anything but title.

I think of this as the pacifist mentality, one that somehow doesn't think we have to fight to keep our companies growing, that doesn't think others will fill the vacuums we create.

Everyone who brags that he or she is a pacifist is really lying. Pacifism is an intellectual deceit perpetrated by those who want to elevate themselves above the average man or woman, to distance themselves from the Great Unwashed.

To this pretentious class of snobs, anyone who favors war—even in defense of liberty—is too much of a dumb slob to understand the pious sanctity of a blanket refusal to go to war.

The reason I say the pacifists are lying is that when an enemy army arrives at their front door, prepared to seize their homes and abscond with their children, they will be the first to call 911—begging the police to dispatch the First Marine Division to their aid. Pacifism doesn't hold up when it leaves the debating society or the ivy-covered halls and confronts reality in a dangerous and uncertain world.

There is a different but equally ridiculous form of pacifism in business. I hear it from those who tell me, ever so haughtily, that they don't want to take market share from others. They simply want to keep what they have and allow the others to have theirs.

This never works. Business is a form of war. Every manager who deceives himself into believing that all parties will play fair should put aside their *Neville Chamberlin Guide to Peace through Submission*, and recognize that, sooner or later, the "nice firm" across town will be on the march, determined to eat their lunch.

The rule of the jungle, for the survivors that is, is "He who acts first, wins." Those sitting on the sidelines pretending that:

- life is fair,
- people will be honorable just because you are, and
- kindness can create and enforce a balance of power

are all delusional. They may trumpet their pacifism, but they won't make it to the boardroom.

Your goal is to build a scalable and sustainable business. The pride of your life's work. The financial engine for you and your family.

In our free enterprise capitalist system, in our exceptional nation, there are no limits beyond those you impose on yourself.

The time has come to declare war and to achieve the outlandish success that can be yours.

Don't wait. The time is now!

About the Author.

Mark Stevens is the CEO of MSCO, a global marketing and management consultancy, and a popular media commentator on a host of business matters, including marketing, branding, management, and sales. Stevens's firm, MSCO, was founded in 1995 and has served a stellar roster of clients including Nike, Starwood, GE, Guardian Life, Intrawest, Estee Lauder, A.I.G., The MONY Group, Environmental Systems Products, Virgin Air, and hundreds of main street businesses. MSCO deploys a proprietary business-building methodology based on capturing customers, amplifying them, and maintaining them for perpetual growth.

The author of two dozen books, including the best-sellers *Your Marketing Sucks* and *Sudden Death: The Rise and Fall of EF Hutton*, Stevens is known for delivering business insights with blunt truths and unconventional wisdom. He is an in-demand speaker at organizations from Wharton to RE/MAX and is a commentator on the Fox Business Network.

Stevens's popular blog, "Unconventional Thinking," is ranked among the "Top 10 Marketing Blogs in the World" by blogged.com.